The World Behind The World

Illustration for Cover

In the Hindu tradition Vishnu reigns as the Supreme Being who creates the universe while dreaming and floating on the cosmic ocean. Vishnu originates all the elements of life and remains present in them, so that each living being remains connected to the god of creation. When the underlying order of the world or "natural law" requires renewal Vishnu incarnates on earth to regenerate existence and put things back in balance.

The first incarnation of the creator god was in the form of a fish called Matsya. The little fish appears to Manu, the ancestor of humanity, and asks for protection from the bigger fishes in the sea. After Manu saves the little fish it grows rapidly, becomes enormous, and eventually saves its human savior from the great flood. In the illustration Vishnu can be seen emerging from the fish and revealing the divine presence to Manu. The story depicts the continuing relationship between the divine essence of life and the smallest creatures of creation with humanity in the middle able to offer a helping hand.

The World Behind The World

Living at the Ends of Time

Much peace and many blessings,

Michael Meade

Michael Meade

GREENFIRE PRESS
An Imprint of Mosaic Multicultural Foundation

GREENFIRE PRESS
An Imprint of Mosaic Multicultural Foundation

Contents

I

The World Behind the World

CHAPTER 1

RUN TOWARDS THE ROAR

Stories are the oldest school for humankind. Genuine stories offer a living school where the only entry requirements are an active imagination, some capacity to feel one's own feelings and a willingness to approach the world as a place of mystery and revelation. Stories are the "imaginal" base of the world, a living literature that underlies and secretly unifies everything. People feel more whole when listening to a story and feel most lost when out of touch with their own story.

Genuine stories don't prove anything. Rather, they reveal things about the world that are already there, but were not being seen. Stories speak the many-minded speech of symbols that convey images and ideas at the same time, in the little time and space it takes to tell a good tale. Stories deal with those things that cannot simply be measured or reduced to "the facts of the matter." Stories concern things that matter more than simple facts can ever tell. A real story is an installment of eternity.

The world, despite its disasters, tragedies and villainies, can't end unless it runs out of stories. For this world is made of stories, each tale a part of an eternal drama being told from beginning to end and over again. As long as all the stories don't come to an end the world will continue.

That's what I tell young people when they ask if this world will end soon. And increasingly, young people ask about the end of the world. Whether it be educated youth considering the dangers of global warming and climate change, less privileged ones who feel the bite of poverty and the growing disparity between rich and poor, or those exposed to the increased threats of violence and extremism—modern youth grow up amidst threats of natural disaster and nightmares of terrorism and can't help but doubt the future of the world.

Increasingly, it seems that The End can come at any moment, either from a mistake of culture or an accident of nature. Scientific theories and religious myths seem to echo each other as both statistics and scriptures predict apocalyptic conditions on earth. Nature and culture, so long divided and seemingly opposed, finally find each other again at the point of imminent annihilation. The Uncertainty Principle that has come to rule science also becomes the common mood of the people. And youth, who are expected to question their own future, come to question whether there will be any future at all.

Typically youth carry the unfolding dream of life; so it's startling to hear young people wondering whether the world will wait for them to find their way into it. When the end seems near everyone can feel old; even the young become older than they should be. What story are we in when those carrying the dream of life increasingly find themselves near the doors of death?

In this world, life and death both roar at the frailty of the individual soul and it's easy to become prey to fear of either one or the other. As fears about the world accumulate and terrors abound, I often recall an old African teaching about fear. On the ancient savannahs life pours forth in the form of teeming, feeding herds. Nearby, lions wait in anticipation of the hunt. They send the oldest and weakest member of the pride away from the hunting pack. Having lost most of its teeth, its roar is far greater than its ability to bite. The old one goes off and settles in the grass across from where the hungry lions wait.

As the herds enter the area between the hunting pack and the old lion it begins to roar mightily. Upon hearing the fearful roar most of the herd turn and flee from the source of the fear. They run wildly in the opposite direction. Of course, they run right to where the strongest lions of the group wait in the tall grass for dinner to arrive. "Run towards the roar," the old people used to tell the young ones. When faced with great danger run towards the roaring, for there you will find some safety and a way through.

The threat of the end of the world being near can be viewed as an old lion that has roared many times before. People have always feared The End. Fear of the end of the world has been there from the very beginning of it. The End has been repeatedly predicted and religiously expected, yet has never arrived. Sometimes the greatest safety comes from going to where the fear seems to originate. Facing The End may be the best way to begin again. Amidst the roaring of the threatened and troubled world, surprising ways to begin it all again may wait to be found.

THE LIONS OF THE MOMENT

These days the roaring of The End seems to have more teeth than usual as both nature and culture tend to unravel before us and paths to safety seem impossible to find. The relentless effects of mass cultures and the blindness increasingly found in mass religions threaten to divide the earth into explosive factions fueled by winds of fear, the fury of raw emotions, and the recklessness of fixed beliefs. Humans stand in amidst increasing tensions, exposed on one side to the raw energies of human greed and dangerous creeds while exposed on the other to the invisible rays of a once friendly sun.

It's a time of great change and many things do come to an end. Yet, those who run away from the roar of the world tend to run straight into the teeth of the many "isms" that promise to remove all doubts and deliver either safety or salvation. The lions of the contemporary moment include fundamentalism and nihilism, literalism and cynicism, scientism and various forms of "saviorism."

Caught between growing fears and deepening terrors, mankind suffers a loss of imagination as well as a narrowing of ideas. Everything seems to polarize into fundamental oppositions between religions, generations, genders, races, classes, and ideologies. Hard issues harden and hard attitudes prevail. Faced with an increasing tension at the level of existence many turn to fundamentalist beliefs and fixed ideologies in order to escape the presence of great uncertainty.

Whereas old apocalyptic visions involved a wrathful god or an offended pantheon of deities wiping clean the slate of creation, current imaginings increasingly place the dangers of total destruction in the hands of mankind. Having lost most "technologies of the sacred," humans increasingly turn to man-made inventions and technological advances that might blow everything to kingdom come.

Instead of god punishing his creatures for straying, something inside humanity becomes the source of destruction. In a sense, mankind has become a force of nature as the new apocalypse involves an imminent sense of self-destruction as well as forms of nihilism that diminish the sense of earthly wonder once natural to the human soul.

Whether it be mankind as the generating force behind global warming or "man's inhumanity to man" converted to nuclear disaster, humankind seems to have a greater hand than usual in the sense of the end being near. On one hand this involves a "negative inflation" in which mankind assumes powers typically assigned to god or the gods. On the other hand, it points to a greater awareness of the crucial role of humanity in the delicate balance of the cosmic dance of life.

Fear and terror grow through the de-spiriting and diminishing of our sense of the earth as part of an eternal and enduring world. By missing the wonder and beauty of the earth, we increase the terror in it. When nothing is holy anymore, all can become a holy terror. Terror grows where fears are not faced and entered into, where instincts and intuitions are denied in favor of abstract ideas, fixed beliefs, and ideologies. By fearing fear and not running towards the roar, people create the space for blind terror to grow.

As a poet once said, "A false sense of security is the only kind there is." Those who seek security in a rapidly changing world run right into the teeth of one dilemma or another. It might be better to run towards the roar and learn what it means to live in a time of many endings. In the end the only genuine security can be found in taking the risks that the soul would take. For the old soul in the human psyche knows that the whole thing has hung by a thread all along.

Fear is an old word that derives from the same roots as "fare," as in "thoroughfare." Although it often causes people to run away, *fear* means "to go through it." Fear used to be called "the awakener," for healthy fear intends to awaken the soul and guide it to greater connections to the living Soul of the World. The hidden purpose of fear involves bringing us closer to inner resources and a greater knowledge of what carries us throughout life. In the end, what we fear will not go away, for it indicates what we must *go through* in order to live more fully. Facing fears of the end of the world can begin to open ways of going on to where all seems destined to end.

In story terms, the end always involves a loose thread or last chance that turns everything around. When it seems that the end is near, the best way to help the world involves learning the threads of story that are woven into the soul to begin with. Learning and living out the risks the soul would take has always been the greatest security for humanity. The conditions in which we find ourselves are the conditions through which we must find our true selves and the dream threaded into our lives from before it began.

The real risk in this life has always been that of becoming oneself amidst the uncertainties of existence. In the end all we can offer the world is the life we came here to live. That's the way of this world: safety is found where living in meaningful ways has been fully risked. When it seems that the end is near and all might be lost, running towards the roar means entering the struggle to preserve the beauty and meaning of individual lives as well as grasping the wonder of the world itself.

In living the life the soul came to earth to live a person automatically contributes to the meaning and continuance of life on earth. When the end comes the only thing people have to offer is the tale of how they struggled to live the life the soul intended. All the rest is the roaring and wailing of unlived energies.

While eruptions in nature and disruptions of culture tend to produce nightmare scenarios and apocalyptic visions, something deep in the soul of humanity also responds to the roaring of the end. Great crises and impossible demands often provoke hidden resources and reveal hints of the underlying wholeness and unity of life. The threat of collapse and utter loss can also provoke a deeper sense of wholeness where nothing but our total involvement and whole-heartedness will work.

The point of "apocalypse now" may be a deeper initiation of the creative self within each person. When everything outside tends to fall apart the hidden unity inside life may be closer to the surface and calling for attention. The West, so dedicated to the outer world, may find more solace through revelations of the deep Self within and the underlying, in-dwelling sense of a unifying principle and guiding force in each life.

In the midst of radical changes in nature and the rattling of cultural institutions the point may be to turn again to the inner realm where old practices and deep awareness can produce moments of wholeness. When the whole thing seems about to fall apart revelations of the deep Self within may be closer than ever. Rather than the need to save the whole world, the real work of humanity may be to find some wholeness within.

BECOMING ANCIENT AGAIN

Amidst the rapid changes and reckless speed of life something ancient and knowing keeps trying to catch up to us. While we rush about, losing time all the time, something timeless tries to get our attention. When we finally run out of time we might finally turn to timeless things again and find the sources of unity and wholeness that hide within the limits of literal time. In the end the old ideas and the ancient ways of knowing try to catch up and help humanity as well as the world survive.

Something ancient was rooted in this world from the very beginning. What we call "the world" has always been old; oldness has been part of it all along. Like so many things in this old world the roots of the word *world* divide in two. One root comes from *wer* meaning woman or man. The other root rises from *old* meaning "grown," as in "grown up," especially as in ripened and fully grown. On one level the world evolved as it grew up. On another level it was fully there, fully manifest, ripened and bearing fruit from the very beginning. Call it paradise, call it a paradox; the world was old and ripe to begin with and something ancient dwells in the human soul as well.

Seen with the eye of imagination this world is an old woman or an old man. Oldness and the sense of an indwelling person have been part of the world all along. Oldness is essential to the presence of the world and anything new in it rests upon the oldness of it. New ideas rise from old radical roots hidden in the ancient ground of being. Anything truly original must touch the origins in order to begin. The world survives because it is old and threaded through with things that last, like last chances and lasting ideas.

Despite the modern fascination with newness and obsessions with the appearance of youth, to be fully grown means to grow properly old, to grow close enough to the origins of life as to become ancient again. Whatever survives the ravages of time and the threats of extinction involves the Old Mind, the instinctive, intuitive inheritance of humankind, the primordial sense of life that permeates all of history without believing in any of it.

The basic split in human life from which so much conflict and anguish develops is a separation from the primordial sense of being, a loss of meaningful connection from the old mind and ancient soul within. "Primordial" refers to the prime sources, the original orders that were present at the beginning and remain hidden at the center of everything, even oneself. When it seems that the end is near the origins of life are also closer. When seen through the old ideas of many cultures, endings and beginning are both mythical occasions, both close to the place of origins and to the sources of originality.

All new inventions depend upon the ancient powers of imagination and creation. To be "original" means to be connected to the origins, to the potentials of the beginning and the ever-inventive, renewing capacity of the Old Mind within. Not the "old brain," but the inner ancestor and ancient companion of the soul with whom we have a hidden but indelible connection. Each person feels more weary of life and more tired of the world when distant from the vital wellspring and fecund mud of the Old Mind within. People can lose their minds if the hidden patterns and unifying threads held by the ancient knower within become overly frayed or severed.

The same fate can befall a culture that turns away from the ancient and ancestral energies that have always managed to find paths of survival and ways of renewal. For, it is the Old Mind within that knows that "there is nothing new under the sun;" that even the latest thing must be newly shaped from something old to begin with. In the end there are no new problems, only the same ancient issues of existence arranged in puzzling new ways.

WHAT THE OLD MIND HAS IN MIND

The Old Mind exists within each person, an inner language written in the bones, lodged in ancient longings that won't abandon life, speaking through dreams that drift through dark prisons towards secret dawns that wash the streets of history clean and leave traces of gold mixed with the ruins of time. The Old Mind is the ancient, Adam-naming mind already connected to the Soul of the World and confident of its home in the earthly realm.

What I'm calling the Old Mind is a knowing presence within, a pre-systematic and primordial awareness that includes instincts for survival and intuitions of creation. The Old Mind is archaic and immediate; it connects to the elemental forces of the earth and to the organic energies of the body. Through connections to the Old Mind we participate in the life of the soul, and become an "old soul" capable of knowing again ideas that live in the blood and images that keep this old world going despite and because of its troubles.

A hidden wholeness underlies the entire project of creation, yet we only know it when we allow ourselves to slip behind the veil that separates the outer world from the inner life. When in touch with the Old Mind within we become original, more genuinely instinctive, intuitively closer to the origins of life and available to the inner movements of creation. In the Old Mind creation is ongoing. The Old Mind is both ancient and immediate and it has something in mind for us. It already knows all the plots and paths life can take. Yet it wants to see the whole thing played out again and again with the next unique twist and with all the grandeur and restless, reckless abandon native to the human heart.

Something ancient and wise keeps trying to catch up to us, but can only do so when we slow down enough and turn away from the manic rush at the surface of life. Turning back and looking inward allows the inner indigenous to catch up with our contemporary self. In the eternal Lascaux of the Old Mind, life slows downward and ancient ways of imagining and perceiving the world can light a way in the dark again.

The Old Mind remains connected to the second chances in life and to inner resources able to help renew life from the source of being. It offers second chances, again and again. To any who would listen, it says: "You can't help but be who you are... and where." From that small notion of awareness and implicit motion of forgiveness, the Old Mind offers a thousand ways to step further into life and begin the whole thing again. For, the Old Mind is also the Beginner's Mind that provides endless ways to start over no matter what mistakes have been made along the way. It is the Original Mind that returns things to their origins and keeps finding original ways to survive the disasters of life and learn anew.

The Old Mind lives on meaning and thrives on mystery; it whispers of a mythical presence woven from the beginning in each soul. It is the mind within the brain, the heart within the heart. It speaks of the poetic unity and secret history hidden in humanity. For there is a mind behind the brain, one that carries messages between brain and heart and allows thought and feeling to meet. The Old Mind is the sage in the heart.

The Old Mind is both indigent and indigenous; it wanders about and feels at home anywhere; for its home is everywhere and nowhere at once. When in touch with it we think as our ancestors did; we find new versions of old stories, become prototypical instead of typecast and become available to the greater dramas of life and love. The Old Mind is the source of purpose and calling in each life. Despite modern confusions about individual purpose and meaning in life, the Old Mind has destinations and destinies in mind for us.

The Old Mind is the old soul in each person, the ancient lord hidden in the self, the wise old woman taking up the loom of life again and again. The Old Mind is full of paradises and paradoxes. It likes to puzzle over the same old puzzling things, again and again. It thrives on both continuity and surprise. The Old Mind is "god-struck," struck by the divine in this world again and again, able to see something holy in every detail of life. When we allow it to operate in us, we become more vital; we see the world as standing up alive and talking to us and giving us the responsibility of joining in and talking back and lending a helping hand.

The Old Mind is what connects a person to the dream of life and to the song of nature. It's the old poetic mind, eternally threaded to the animated, animistic, altruistic, and ever abundant Soul of the World. The Old Mind penetrates and fecundates the smallest details of life as well as the grandest thoughts we have of the world. It reaches to the depths of the earth and to the expanse of the Milky Way. It's connected to the Chain of Being and the promise of life, it's emboldened by the presence of love and longings that remember the touch of the divine.

Did I mention that the Old Mind likes to exaggerate? The Old Mind is part of human nature and it indulges in excesses at every turn in the same way that Nature fashions untold species and tosses up whole forests where some might expect a simple tree and revels in flocks of birds that obscure the sky and beasts that turn the plains alive. The Old Mind is naturally abundant with ideas and images, with dreams and schemes and plot twists that prolong both the agonies and delights of existence on this old earth.

In the Age of Reason the Old Mind seems too illogical and irrational; yet it is the first way of being in the world, the original way of knowing anything of the world. The ancient mind is logical in its own ways. It is mythological, psychological, and ultimately cosmological. The Old Mind sings the eternal song, the hymn of creation continually whispering through the lips of time. It finds ways to weave new life from death, just as whole forests erupt from the thread-dark roots of fallen trees.

The Old Mind is dedicated to the strange persistence of Once Upon a Time, the mythical, mystical thread upon which everything hangs in the end. The exact medicine for the isolation and dissociation so characteristic of the modern mind lies in finding again the ancient wellsprings of human thought and the underlying continuity that persists within the old soul and tries to catch up to us at every crossroads in life.

OLD SOULS AND THE ETERNAL YOUTH

The Old Mind includes the eternal youth hidden in the heart of the elders as well as the old soul trying to awaken in the heart of each youth. When the oldest and the youngest capacities of the soul come together, then we have finally caught up with ourselves. Then, we can learn again how to hold the ends and beginnings of this world together.

It used to be said that genuine culture is made from the dreams of youth and the visions of elders. The arc of imagination that secretly generates and sustains human culture stretches between the eternal youth dreaming on the story of life and the old soul envisioning paths of survival and ways of wisdom. The dream of life on earth requires the genius of youth and the wisdom of the elders and a meaningful conversation between the two. For, each holds a key to the true imagination of the course of human life.

When cultures fall apart it happens in two places at once: where its youth are rejected and where its elders are forgotten. Modern cultures tends to have a mass of "olders" but a dearth of elders. That leaves youth more isolated and alone at the extremes of life; more available to tragic deaths and wasted lives than they would normally be. Youth are at greater than necessary risk when their olders fail to become genuine elders and try not to be at risk at all.

Secretly youth and elders relate through a sense of timelessness, though intensities of imagination, through proximity to the extremes of life. Youth and elders stand at the opposite extremes of the arc of imagination that sparks between beginning and end. When the end seems near the dreams of youth and the visions of the elders are both required in order to run towards the roar and find some safety and ways to continue the world.

In traditional cultures the elders would gather the stories of life and death and the mythic tales that stir and sustain the core images and ideas of human cultures. The elders were expected to hold the ends together with the beginnings in order to bridge this world with the otherworld while inviting youth into the eternal drama and ongoing dance of life. That used to be a specialty of the elders, before people began to believe that old simply means over the hill and on the downward side of life. Genuine knowledge, they used to say when people still considered "gnosis" more important than simple belief, makes a person older; not just aged but wiser in the ways of the roaring world.

As the threats to existence become more evident and more threatening many people feel driven by the urgency to interrupt the reckless course of events. Others begin to feel hopeless and defeated by forces so much greater than the frail and frequently misguided presence of humankind. Yet, the elders of older cultures often suggested slowing down to allow the inner companion and Old Mind in the soul to catch up.

Real solutions to short-term thinking and disposable ideas involve long thoughts and ancient intuitions that reach all the way from the seeming ends of time to the roots of the eternal. When it seems that there's no time left at all, it's time for the eternal connections to be rediscovered. Behind all the roaring and confusion of this world the otherworld of imagination and living spirit waits to be found again. The "world behind the world" remains the source of all that appears in the earthly realm and the place where solutions for its raging problems must be sought.

Although the current problems are urgent and undeniable, rushing for solutions may not allow the best chance for truly creative answers to be found. It's like the young seeker who set out into the world and wound up in a certain temple. He began to study in the ways of that place, especially the practice of meditation. Soon he was meditating day and night, barely stopping his practice to eat or sleep. As time went on he grew thin and continually seemed to be on the verge of complete exhaustion.

The teacher of that temple advised the student to slow down, to rest and take better care of himself. The young seeker ignored the advice, even intensified his practice. One day the teacher asked: "Why are you rushing so much? What is the great hurry?" The answer of the devotee came back quickly: "I am after enlightenment and there is no time to waste."

The teacher considered that idea and responded, "How do you know that enlightenment is running before you, so that you must rush after it? What if enlightenment is actually trying to catch up to you. What if you must become more still for awareness and wisdom to find you where you already are? What if all your haste and feverish determination have actually been your habit of running away from it?"

During the radical upheavals in the Renaissance period of Western culture, people used to say: Festina lente—make haste slowly. In Africa where connections to animal intelligence remain vital, they offer the proverb that suggests: One more day won't rot the elephant.

When the issues become huge and heavy like an elephant, rushing ahead without a genuine vision of where to go indicates a lack of wisdom as well as an excess of fear. As people used to say; when the troubles become overwhelming and even prayers don't work, then it's time for a story. Stories help everyone, young and old to hold the ends together with the beginnings.

CHAPTER 2

HOLDING THE THREAD OF LIFE

There's an old tribal tale, a little folk myth about what happens when everything seems to fall apart, when the world diminishes in beauty and the threads of existence seem about to be cut. It's a story held over from the time when people learned directly from the earth, when the earth was speaking to the people and folks knew better how to listen. In those earlier times people considered the earth itself to be a living story, a veritable storehouse of knowledge as well as an abundant natural resource.

People at that time told of a cave in which knowledge of the world and how to best live in it could be found. Even now, some of the old people say that the cave exists and might be found again. They say it's tucked away in the side of some mountain. Not too far to go they say, yet no one seems to find it anymore. Despite all the highways and byways, all the thoroughfares and back roads that crosscut the face of the earth; despite all the maps that detail and define each area, no one seems to find that old cave anymore.

It's too bad, they say, because inside the cave can be found genuine knowledge about the essential conditions of this world, about how the earth can become threatened and troubled and how to act when those dark dramas might be occurring again.

Inside the cave there lives an old woman who remains unaffected by the rush and confusion and strife of daily life. She attends to other things and spends most of her time weaving. She wants to fashion the most beautiful garment in the whole world and she has been at that weaving project for a long time. She has reached the point of making a fringe for the edge of her exquisite cloak. She wants that fringe to be special, wants to weave it with porcupine quills.

She likes the idea of using something that could poke you as an element of beauty; she likes turning things around and seeing life in unusual ways. The old woman must flatten each quill with her teeth. From years of biting down on porcupine quills her teeth have become worn down to nubs that barely rise above her gums. Still, the old woman keeps biting down and keeps weaving on.

She only interrupts her work to stir the soup that simmers in a great cauldron at the back of the cave. The cauldron hangs over a fire that began a long time ago. The old woman can't recall anything older than that fire; it might be the oldest thing there is in this world. Occasionally she does recall that she must stir the soup in the cauldron that hangs over it. That soup contains all the seeds and grains and herbs that sprout up over the surface of the earth. If the old woman doesn't stir the ancient stew once in a while, the fire will scorch the ingredients and there's no telling what troubles could result from that.

So the old woman divides her efforts between weaving the exquisite cloak and stirring the elemental soup. In a sense, she's responsible for weaving things together as well as for stirring everything up. She senses when the time has come to let the weaving go and stir things up again. Then, she leaves the weaving on the floor of the cave and turns to stirring the soup. Because she is old and tired from her labors and from the relentless passage of time, she moves slowly and it takes a while for her to amble over to the cauldron.

As the old woman shuffles across the floor and makes her way to the back of the ancient cave, a black dog watches her every move. The dog was there all along, seemingly asleep; yet suddenly awake as soon as the old weaver turns her attention from one task to the other. As she becomes busy stirring the soup, the black dog goes to where the weaving lies on the floor of the cave.

The dog picks up a loose thread with its teeth and begins to pull on it. Since each thread has been woven to another, pulling upon one begins to undo them all. As the great stew is being stirred up, the elegant garment comes undone.

When the old woman returns to take up her handiwork, she finds a chaotic mess instead. The garment woven with such care has been roughly pulled apart; the fringe all undone. The elegance of creation has been turned to a mess of destruction. The old woman stands quietly and looks upon the remains of her once beautiful design. She ignores the presence of the black dog and stares intently at the tangle of undone threads and distorted patterns.

After a while, she bends down, picks up a loose thread and carefully begins to weave the whole thing again. As she pulls thread after thread from the chaotic mess before her she begins to imagine again the most beautiful garment in the whole world. As she weaves, new designs appear before her and her old hands give shape to them. Soon she has forgotten what she wove before as she concentrates on making this the most beautiful garment in all the world.

THE CAVE OF KNOWLEDGE

Upon hearing the tale, most people feel sympathy for the old woman who labors so long and hard only to wind up having to start everything all over again. What a shame that she can't finish her work; how unfair and punishing this world can be. Most feel that if the black dog would just stop causing trouble and undoing everything, the old woman could complete her weaving. Then this world would be a proper place and the old woman could finally rest. Then it would be "her time" and she could enjoy the fruits of her labor.

The old people of the tribe see the story differently. They take solace in the strange tale of the cave and in the way the old woman faces the mess and deals with disaster. They recall the old weaver in the cave when times turn hard, when the world seems to become darker and they have to face some chaos and confusion again. The old people see the deliberate workings of the Old Mind inside the story.

The old people say that the persistent weaver is really the Old Woman of the World herself. They identify the stew with all the seeds of the earth as the living soup of creation that needs to be stirred up again and again. They point out that trouble and turmoil are the ways in which this world changes and that Nature itself is ever changing, always cooking something up and shape-shifting and starting things over again.

They say the fire in that cave is actually the necessary flame burning at the center of the green-garmented earth. They know that the cave holding the hidden weaving of life is the world itself, the wondrous earth with its great creations and shining garments that slip over the naked presence of life; the fecund, seething earth with its stew of living seeds, with its troubles boiling and bubbling away, with its ancient sacred fire hidden at the very core.

The old people consider that the garment being woven again and again with beauty and care is the world itself. They make the point that should the old woman ever complete the design, then the whole world would come to an end. The old people see the troubles of this world from a different angle. Being closer to death than most, they have a deeper sense of the unraveling of life. And, they like a little story that can be used to consider such big things. They like how it brings out many issues using only a few threads. They like the economy of that and the way it can save time when there seems to be little time left.

Be thankful for the trouble in this world and for the black dog that occasionally unravels the whole thing, they say. For the black dog acts out the role of time that eventually undoes and dismantles everything made in this world. They remind us that the nature of this world requires that the beauty of it be lost, that it be rediscovered and lost again, that the eternal patterns of it become forgotten in order to be relearned, that the designs of life be recast over and over again.

It's a simple story, but a favorite with the elders who stay close to the presence of the Old Mind. They relate to the struggles of the old woman, especially to the place where she must face the mess that remains after all her best efforts have been thoroughly undone. Being older, they have lived through many tragedies and survived many disasters. They have seen how life can be wasted and how blood can be foolishly spilled on the earth. They have witnessed the darkness that people bring to the weaving of the histories of the world.

The elders know that the black dog so dedicated to undoing things belongs to the Old Woman of the World just as much as that garment woven of beauty. They have suffered the loss of many dreams and have had to learn how to start all over again. Having suffered in the middle of the mess of life they have learned to see with a "darkened eye," see in ways that can hold the ends and beginnings of life together. When the end seems near again a darker knowledge of the world is needed if creative ways to weave the threads of existence would be found again.

The old people know that the "black dog times" come around again and again and require that the living people find a new vision for life or else become undone where the threads of nature loosen and the designs of culture collapse. They try to learn from the Old Woman who is also the world itself. They try to gather hints of the new weaving in the midst of the latest unraveling. Whenever things seem completely undone and the whole thing about to end, they recall the old stories and try to imitate the way Nature uses and reuses, cycles and recycles everything and how culture can learn again to do the same.

Hearing the story, some modern people ask: "Is the cave real or something made up?" The old people answer: "Yes." For everything real in this world is also made up; everything real made from "whole cloth" and all of it hanging by a thread all the way along. Those arguments about creation versus evolution miss the point that this world is beginning and ending all the time. Anyone who would have it all one way is simply setting the stage for the black dog to return.

Reality appears where the weft of time is thrown over the warp and weird of eternity. Everything real must be made up from hidden threads that secretly tie it to the unseen, to the world that's behind the world. Each thing that appears and each person that exists is a part of a story delicately woven with the threads of time and eternity, ever on the point of creation and always on the edge of unraveling and slipping back into chaos. That's the world and we all live there.

BLACK DOG TIMES

The black dog demonstrates how all notions of reality and all claims about the facts of life are bare threads that can unravel right before your eyes when the time comes for a radical loosening or a big change. It may be good enough to stick to the facts when things are running smoothly, but in the "black dog times" it becomes necessary to see past the obvious, to glimpse behind the scenes where the soup of life gets stirred up, where destruction and creation change places.

People say, "Beware, the End is coming;" yet it's already here. This world is full of endings; it ends all the time. We live within a life-sized weaving that can unravel before our very eyes. A hurricane can do that, a sandstorm can obliterate the landscape, or someone declares a war and soon everything falls apart.

Forget good intentions, the mess is all around and everyone contributes to it. Most people pretend they don't own a black dog, yet inside their lives things become torn and frayed. The evidence of the inner darkness can be found with our children, ex-spouses, ex-lovers, former friends, and current enemies. At some level, everyone knows it. Our own lives fall apart repeatedly; our best laid plans become blatant disasters.

Then again the soul learns more from failure than from success; in facing up to difficulties it learns of hidden resources and deep resolves within. It learns the darkened knowledge required when it comes time to let the current design go in order to pick up some loose threads and start the life project over again. Dark knowledge includes the lessons learned from loss and the wisdom gathered from surviving our own troubles. Those who learn their own darkness and accept the sorrow of the world become more able to handle the chaos when it all falls apart.

"Each increase of knowledge is an increase of sorrow," says the Old Woman. For genuine knowledge is tinged with the sorrow of the world and touching that makes the soul older, not simply wiser but more ancient. Those who don't come to know, especially to know themselves, remain wet behind the ears no matter their age may be. "Dry souls are best," says the Old Woman, especially when the floods of change come and the black dog starts pulling things apart again.

When it seems that things might end most people become shortsighted and self-involved. Fearing some final emptiness they cling to possessions and become possessed by narrow ideas and fixed beliefs. Yet paying attention to how things end can teach people to become "old like the world" and ancient enough to find ways to survive and even assist creation. That's what many old stories imply and they have survived for ages and lived to tell the tale.

Those who adjust their vision to the unraveling of the world and learn to see with a darkened eye can more quickly find some loose threads to work with and invent ways to join the Old Woman at her endless work of reweaving this old world. In the end, the point is to become a little ancient, to become more mythic and thus original again and find lasting threads amongst the loose ends and last things.

Once the black dog pulls a thread loose something must come to an end, a period of making reaches its conclusion, an era expires. People fear that the final end has come. In the midst of the loss and confusion the cosmic soup gets stirred again. Eventually, life settles down to a simmer and continues albeit differently arranged. The seeds of life have been preserved, but the "world as we know it" has become undone.

STIRRING THE SOUP OF EXISTENCE

"A woman's work is never done," says the Old Woman of the world who has maintenance work to do as well as creative work. If she neglects to "stir things up" the stew of existence boils over, the earth becomes overheated, the seeds of life might burn. The old story depicts it as a simple matter of shifting from one task to another, yet it also implies a cosmic turn. As above so below; as below so above; everything secretly woven together and everything coming somewhat undone when the time for that comes.

Yet it all happens within the greater mystery of continuance. Life is a constant re-creation at the edges of destruction. In the cave of existence each moment creates, destroys, and sustains life. That's the world when seen in its mythic proportions and its mystical reach. When it comes to endings and beginnings the soul turns mythical and mystical in order to grasp the nature of change and glimpse the world that exists behind and beyond the mundane shape of things.

In the cave of the Old Woman we can peek in on the "routines of eternity" and see the three-step dance of the endless drama of the incarnated world. Create, maintain, destroy goes the song of life as it takes three to do the tango of existence. Nature and culture both dance to those steps and share in those eternal motions.

Despite the contemporary fixation on rational thought and the limited world of facts and measurements, the human soul is mythic by nature and mystical by inclination. Despite the amassing of trivial data in the age of information, the soul still dreams in designs that reflect the frailty and beauty of the world as well as the wonders of creation. Amidst the fascination with new technologies and the flood of clever gadgets the old mind recognizes when the world is turning a cosmic corner and everything must shift and change in order to survive.

The Old Woman is connected to the dreaming mind, the inner mine abundantly veined with the gold of imagination. Her cave is also the salt mine that helps preserve life and add flavor to the stew of existence. She can appear as Old Salt Woman who preserves life and meaningful forms of knowledge. She also appears as the moon that rides through the sore darkness of Being; overlooked by those dedicated solely to the light of day. She sits soul-like at the edge of awareness; ever reflective and carefully observant as time's clumsy servants rush back and forth on the narrow roads of history.

The Old Woman is the Old Mind in each person, the persistent creative force that makes life and even love possible; for she loves life and all the mess it makes over and over again. She is Old Mother Nature and the source of all nurture as well. She nurtures each culture through the milk of enduring ideas and creative patterns. She rocks the world in the underlying, archetypal, and original shapes that can hold endings and beginnings together.

She knows the dance of life and the place of death; knows the three-step waltz of creation, maintenance, and destruction. She understands the importance of the unraveling as well as the necessity of the reweaving. Her cave is nowhere and everywhere; it's nowhere to be found and it exists wherever we are when we allow the Old Mind to awaken within us.

The Old Mind is the story-mind that knows how things turn around in the last minute; that knows how the last can become first in the cosmological song and dance of time and eternity. Eternity loves it when things unravel a bit and the veils slip off the time-bound shapes and reality becomes a little thin again. In the great loosening and lifting of the veil between one world and the other the divine becomes revealed again; not the simple revelation of The End, but the surprising renewal of the whole affair again.

As the Black Dog awakens, so does the Old Mind that has been trying to reconnect to the troubled soul of humanity. Just as the Black Dog faithfully does its job of unraveling the productions of time, the Old Mind tries to return some genuine imagination to the human soul. The Old Mind knows the ways that life renews and doesn't mind either the loss of forms or the making of new shapes from old cloth. It has all happened before and each time it came to The End before starting again.

To be alive when it all seems about to end means to be near the lifting of the veil. For *apocalypse*, so often used to proclaim the final, fiery end means to lift the veil between one thing and another. Apocalyptic times involve both uncovering and discovering; both closures and disclosures. Being alive at this time means to be caught in the loosening of both culture and nature and the undoing of many common patterns. Yet, it also means to be near the threads of existence and invited to the great reweaving of the garment of life.

In times of many endings it becomes important to have a sense for lasting things, a narrative feel for life, and a reverence for the unseen. In the end, or near it, the real issue isn't the future of humanity, but the presence of eternity.

Some say that this world is a virgin that should be left untouched; others say that it is a wise old woman with a nose for trouble, just enough trouble to keep things going. The Old Woman of the World weaves wonders with the threads of nature and culture, turning one into the other and back again. She has all of eternity to weave beauty from unlike things, to re-create from what happens to be left over.

She's the heiress of all leftovers, the queen of the dead and mistress of everything that comes to an end. She is also the mistress of all that continues. She shapes all the costumes for the endless, tragicomic displays of history. Her cave is the tomb we all are headed for and the womb from which we began. When near the fateful issues of our lives we are in her hands, as are all the threads of existence.

We imitate her, each in our own way biting down on life, trying to make something of the threads that pull us secretly along, trying to weave a life from the cross-hairs of fate. She used to be better known as the old triple goddess of Fate who spins and weaves and fixes the threads by which each person and each event becomes set into the tapestry of the world. We all sleep in her cave, fall back there whenever we dream; return there when life has run out its thread.

The Old Woman of the World is part of the human inheritance that resides in the cave of the mind and in the crevices of the heart where the designs of the life wait to be discovered again. When things unravel before our very eyes, when people become lost and the world seems to have lost its bearings, it is lost ideas and ancient imaginations that seek to be found again.

It isn't something completely new that needs to be invented; rather something ancient made new again that holds the promise of survival and a return to the beauty of the world. It is the oldness of the world that allows it to continue. Any real progress must involve the same old elements that were there at the beginning; for they are necessary for any genuine attempt to begin again.

"All of this has happened before, but you have to become old enough to know that," says the Old Woman as she looks upon the chaotic mess that was once the vibrant and elegant garment of the living world. Her only recreation is the re-creation of the world. In the end, when all else fails, she's ready to start the whole thing over again.

Her designs combine ancient forms with new shapes. Her tools are nature and culture, and she is most present where the two intersect and entwine. The sacred, they used to say, occurs where nature and culture meet. The Old Woman reminds that this world is a sacred place made of weaving nature and culture together; that it becomes most thoroughly undone when those two fall too far apart.

The inner nature of humanity connects us to great Nature on one hand and to ancient threads of imagination and genuine culture on the other. Each soul is naturally tied to the two great garments of life on earth. Each is secretly connected to the evergreen thread of Nature that winds and breathes throughout the living world and each threaded to the surprising and enigmatic cloak of culture that adorns the earth with patterns of imagination and displays the frail beauty of humanity.

In the cave of the Old Woman culture and Nature meet as the divine thread of life gets pulled through both. Those who think that human culture must exploit and dominate the blind resources of brute nature miss the point and those who believe that only Nature can lead to salvation miss it going the other way. The point of renewal, the point of exchange where eternity can reverse the march of time can best be found where Nature and culture meet.

EDGE BEINGS, FRINGES OF THE SACRED

The edge of existence remains an unfinished, a living fringe shaped with strands of Nature and threads of culture; always just becoming, often being loosened and rewoven; being re-imagined, realigned, and redesigned. Humans enter at the edge where creation plays with the limits of time and the abundance of eternity. Humans are strung on the chain of being between the animals and the angels, children of the sodden earth, yet pulled on by unseen spirit-threads that lean towards eternity.

Humans are part of the edge of life and the fringe of being. On the cutting edge biologically and sometimes metaphysically, humans are "fringe beings," creatures of the edge, hard to deal with like the porcupine quills that can poke things or become elegant and beautiful. Life bites down on each soul in order to place it properly in the intricate pattern of the garment of the world. We feel that bite as fear and pain, as tragedy and loss, yet it is intended to make us vital and meaningful and to make the world a place of drama and beauty.

Humans are born in the half-light of the cave of knowledge and woven to the edge of creation. Ever on the fringe and just on the verge of awareness; ever in search of the next ray of light that might illuminate the way forward. Humans play out the experiments of fate and destiny on the living edges where the pulse of Nature and the dreams of culture meet. If we survive at all, we do so by virtue of joining the Old Woman and picking up a thread that can wind us more fully into the great dance of life.

At the seeming end of time the fabric of life loosens and the veil between this world and the other becomes thin and tattered. As time seems to be running out the eternal tries to slip back into awareness. Things become both impossible and more possible at the same time. Amidst the feeling of desperate ending, new designs appear. Amidst the loss of certainty and the chaos of theories about how it all might end, the unseen thread of the eternal can be found again. In mythic stories and wisdom tales, in dreams and genuine visions, hidden threads continue to pull at life in surprising and confounding ways and the world goes on.

Each of us is an "old soul" in the depths of our souls; and each is an eternal youth in the wonder of our minds and in the longings of our heart's desire. Each has an innate, if subtle, connection to the Old Mind and to the inner cave of imagination and renewal. Dreams take us there. So does love. And a revelatory idea can do the same. For eternal threads hide within each life story the way dreams hide within the sleeper.

Living at the edge of life makes humanity a bit reckless, somewhat foolish, and sometimes dangerous to the dance of existence. Yet, being open both to this world and to the otherworld makes humans innately creative and necessary to existence. Nature and culture conspire where a person lives out the inherent and inspired threads of their unique inner nature. Those with eyes to see and enough soul to imagine find ways to continue and even intensify the human involvement in the creative experiment of this daylit, night-born world.

The cave of knowledge is an open secret in this life; it's hidden within, often the last place where people look for knowledge of how to enter life more fully. Maybe it's the presence of the black dog that keeps people from searching within. At any rate, the inner cave and storehouse of creative designs waits to be found by those seeking some initiation to the mythic aspects of life and wishing to learn their unique way of being in this world.

When the Black Dog times come around and the world rattles and loosens again, only those young enough to recall eternity and old enough to befriend its surprising presence learn to see with the darkened eye that finds a way though the tangle of endings and beginnings. When the world becomes dark with endings it becomes time to turn to the inner thread that first brought each soul to this life. Although it cannot be found by common observers, as long as we hold the inner thread of being we cannot be completely lost.

CHAPTER 3

THE ONLY DESIGN WE MUST LEARN

Although mostly forgotten since birth became a medical occasion, old ideas held each birth to be an initiation for both mother and child. The mother enacts an initiatory ritual as she suffers and labors to give more life to life, while each newborn child begins its initiatory path with the pangs of birth. Each moment of birth is momentous because it presents an eruption of the eternal entering the time-bound as each soul brings a thread of eternity to the limits of earthly time and place.

After childhood, longings woven into the soul awaken and expects the initiatory path to open again. The real "growing pains" of youth involve the soul's attempts to enter life more fully in order to deliver its innate gifts and sense of purpose to the world. Modern mass cultures become blind to the real meaning of individual life and tend to replace the uniqueness of the individual with statistical categories and the dull expectations of linear time and literal life.

Two feet of the soul walk each of us through the world, one foot continuing the steps of becoming incarnate and the other foot secretly tied to and being pulled by the inner threads of fate and destiny. That's the continuous dilemma of the human soul, to be a limited creature born of time and place and to be a child of the eternal and called to an unseen destiny.

Only through the efforts of the individual soul can the unseen world with its hidden knowledge and unconscious aims become known.

Lifelong initiation is the genuine opus of the soul, the project of and for a lifetime, the genuine work and inherent purpose waiting to be realized within each life. For each is a unique experiment trying to fully incarnate by delivering its inner message to the world. The self or soul can only know itself through the lived "eachness" and hidden "uniqueness" that it brought to life to begin with.

Initiation involves the continuous breaking open of areas of the soul where the inner story waits to become known and to live its way into the world. Each young person already carries a story and seeks both the blessings and troubles required if it is to awaken within them. And, the olders and elders tend to lose their short-term memories in order to recall the inner story with its eternal threads and hidden meanings before they reach the door of death.

At the end of life the question becomes whether or not we have been able to unwind the thread that carried us into this world. Only when the hidden threads of fate and the inner hints of destiny become known can the meaning of a life stand forth with its inherent story revealed and its inner value be confirmed. If the genuine project of a life be lived out in a meaningful way all the twists and turns can be seen to have contributed to the unwinding of the thread of destiny. If not, no amount of outer success can amount to true inner worth and no amount of experience add up to genuine meaning.

In the realm of stories and in the inner windings of the human soul the figures of fate and destiny appear primarily in feminine form. After all, the body begins its journey from single cell to complex being within the womb of a woman and ends its journey, long or short, in the tomb of mother earth. Dust thou art and dust thou will return to when the road of life comes to an end.

Feminine characters figure strongly in tales of fate and where the destiny of a soul becomes revealed. The Old Woman of the World has her cosmic weaving to do, yet she also has an interest in each soul who enters the nets of earthly existence. In another old tale she waits at the entrance of a cave that is also a threshold between the worlds. When people die, they go there. The lifelong journey having come to its inevitable end, the wanderer feels an old longing to join the community of souls on the other side.

Modern people often argue over the issue of an afterlife that continues on the other side this life. Of course, modern people argue over everything as if finding proof of this or that could make the world less mysterious and more predictable. Death is the most predictable thing in this world, yet modern cultures tend to avoid real knowledge of that subject. Philosophy begins with the knowledge of death. That was the old idea, the one that prevailed when philosophy was closer to its original sense of *philo-sophia*, where *philo* meant love and *sophia* meant wisdom.

Sophia was the goddess of wisdom who opened the doors to both the love of genuine knowledge and the knowledge of genuine love. For the heart knows from the beginning what it comes to this world to love and knows what it comes to this world to learn. In the end we are all supposed to become philosophers, both knowers and lovers of our own lives before the doors of death appear before us. The old philosophies suggest that those who learn what their souls truly love in life can meet death with less fear and no anger. Strange to say, but a conscious death is the best proof of a lived life.

Modern thought often considers the death of the body to be the actual end of life, even when the exact moment of death still proves to be an elusive mystery. Older ideas and the imagination of all traditional cultures consider that the soul came from somewhere before it appeared and likely returns to that unseen place again. The body is formed of earth and returns to it, dust to dust, mud to mud, clay to clay. The soul, made of more subtle threads, slips past the gates of mortality, destined for a post-mortem appointment on the other side of life.

After shedding the sheath of the body, the soul continues on and crosses to another realm. There, the old tale continues, the recently departed soul finds itself on a path that soon approaches a cave that seems both tomb and womb. At the threshold of that cave the Old Woman of the World awaits the arrival of the newly deceased.

She recognizes one of her children coming along and perceives the pattern that was woven into that soul at the beginning when the cave was the womb of life and the passage way led to the embodied world of incarnation. Being the old mother of fate she played her part when the weaving of that life began. She pulled the individual thread around which the body first formed and gave it a unique twist. Now she wonders what that soul did with the fine thread of imagination and inspiration that it carried all through its days and nights on earth and how it handled the twists of fate.

The Old Woman knows the hidden design and inner fate that was the intrigue behind the entire visit to the earthly realm. Now that death has cut the body thread and brought a conclusion to the life's fervent fever, it's time to review how that story went, how much of the inner tale became a conscious knowing and a living philosophy. What remains after the remains have been placed in the earth is the shape of the life lived and the tracing out of what was truly learned.

Since the deceased was a child of the earth, the Old Woman weaves the design buried in that soul in the dust and waits to see what the wanderer learned of its placement in the fabric of the world. She traces only half the design, for the life lived was intended to become the other half. Now, the soul must make its mark on the earth again, this time by sketching with whatever understanding it may have gathered from life.

In this primordial art form the inner threads of life become revealed. It's the final test and the only preparation is the life already lived; it's far too late for any procrastination; all that is over. Now, there can be no cheating and it turns out that the real cheaters are those who lived someone else's life. Now, no one has any advantage over others, except the original advantage of being a unique soul on the road of life and death.

The story was there all along, the answer to life's test woven within in outline form from the very beginning. Now, the time has come for laying out the genuine facts of life, the consideration of what happened between the inner self and the outer world. There's no multiple choices in this test; each answer requires lived specifics. Was the life intended the one that was lived? Were the brushes with fate and destiny noticed, accepted, truly struggled with? How did the loving go?

For each soul is bound to love in ways that help reveal the longings carried in the depths of the soul. All attempts at loving help to reveal something of the design hidden in the heart, that whispers in the blood, and sings quietly in the soul. In the end it turns out that there were no small lives, only people too hung up with the worries of the little self or too afraid to follow the thread of existence all the way.

The life project can't proceed without love and each soul's way of loving has virtues that make more sense when seen from the other side. So the Old Woman doesn't follow any abstract or moral system in considering the condition of each soul. She knows too much for that. She knows that morality is a substitute for love. She knows that where love resides there is no need for morality and where there is no love, no morality will persist.

Each life has a certain body and the soul-speech hidden within it. What is hidden within is the design that brought us here. This can't be proven in some overt way, yet the inner terms are the subject of life's frequent tests and the core issue once life is over. There's no school for becoming oneself except allowing the inner life to live its way out. All along the way each person is pulled by hidden threads and subjected to twists of fate that secretly wind close to the core of inner meanings.

At the end of life the question isn't whether people obeyed certain rules or avoided certain vices. At the end, the question is whether or not they found the thread of their inner life often enough to learn the destiny that brought them to this life to begin with. If the soul can match the design of the Old Woman with etchings from life's drama it passes into the cave and on to the trail of the ancestors. If not, it returns to the common world again attached to aspects of the design that went unlived.

Of course, what happens to the soul comprises a great mystery that mere words cannot trace. This tale is just one of many stories that the soul carries and considers along the road of life and death. The point of mythic stories isn't that anyone believe them, more that they help us to remember that each life has an inner pattern and awakening to it adds something valuable to the ongoing tale and endless drama of creation.

We are fashioned with the filaments of eternity and carried by the needle of time. Each soul is woven on the loom of life and held together by a warp thread that makes it unique and purposeful, even if a bit strange and weird. The mythic thread continues to nourish the soul with dreams and intimations of spirit, with inklings of originality and sudden desires for change.

Life tends to unravel and lose all sense and meaning when we wander too far from the ways we are already threaded into the world and shaped by our inner pattern. If we allow the inner thread to pull us, we arrive at the intersections where the limits shaped by our fate bring us to our appointments with destiny. The unique ways in which we are woven and spun help us to find our own way and to last in this world.

The soul thread is the most supple, subtle, and determined thing in us, yet the least known aspect of our lives. It is the vitality of our soul dreaming us along and lingering at the edge of our waking. It is the hidden, determined chord at the core of the heart, the thread of song that keeps the rhythm of our life. At times of awakening it becomes the thread that connects the mind with the heart.

While holding to the inner pattern and innate rhythms, all the moments of our lives make sense; without those guides all can seem accidental and pointless. The thread of Fate and the song of eternity entwine within us; both the dark presence of death and the golden thread of life. We risk suffering a "fate worse than death" when we refuse to suffer the fate woven in our soul to begin with.

The invisible inner thread used to be known as the cord of initiation for it secretly pulls us farther into life than we might choose to go on our own. Although not a predetermined or fixed fate it carries a subtle sense of purpose and lends specific direction to each life. Because it cannot be seen or examined in simple ways, modern cultures tend to dismiss its presence. Yet, when the world rattles and everything turns upside down, holding to the inner thread may be the surest way to find meaning and gain a sense of purpose.

Upavita was an old Sanskrit term for the ancient and immediate thread of eternity that runs invisibly through all of life. It was also the name of the sacred thread that hung from the left shoulder of young initiates, worn as a visible reminder of the unseen world and the innate connection of each life to the realm of spirit. The *upavita* was imagined as the red thread of passion that runs within the blood of everything that breathes and as the green thread of existence dancing through the endless windings of the vegetal world. It is the vine of eternity that secretly supports the trees and sends the roots down and winds the living tendrils that connect the Garden of Eden to each blade of graveyard grass.

When worn by initiates it represents the capacity to die the little deaths that make a greater and more conscious life possible. It represents the hidden eternity wihtin each life and the capacity of all persons to awaken to how and where they are threaded to the chain of being. The *upavita* was the holy thread used to indicate that each life was sacred and that becoming conscious meant taking on sacred tasks in the world. Unless a person learns of the sacred intentions in their own life it will be difficult for them to understand the sacred presence in all of life.

The initiatory thread used to be draped across the shoulder of the young so that it fell over the heart and marked them as one seeking a meaningful path that could open the mysteries of that heart. The thread of initiation would be placed by elders who had found some sense of the direction in their own lives and the hidden connections that make the world a place of reverence and meaning and beauty. The older ones would attempt to tie the young seekers to the vital threads of nature and to the living imagination and genuine practices of conscious culture.

Although modern cultures see mostly a generation gap between the old and the young, traditional cultures saw a hidden thread of meaning suspended between the two. If those who are older have found meaning and purpose in the course of their lives they have something meaningful to offer to those just stepping onto the paths of initiation. If those who are younger feel invited into the mysteries of life and death they gain a more immediate reverence for ways to approach the world and their place within it.

In modern cultures relations between elders and youth begin with the idea that they are barely contemporary. Too much time stands between the two and everything changes so quickly that they can hardly relate as contemporaries. They are on opposite sides of the times in which they live and can't see eye to eye.

Modern life encourages a "generation gap" in which the fear between youth and elders grows and each seems to threaten the existence of the other. The rebelliousness of the young opposes the fixed attitudes of the aged; the raw power of youth threatens the fragility of the aged. Youth are too fast, too foolish, too risky and too inconsiderate, while the old are too slow, too limited and too limiting; both too firm and too infirm for the spirit of youth.

Yet, when the old and young truly converse, end and beginning are reconstituted, tradition and innovation are embodied and a subtle renewal of life becomes possible. Something old and meaningful, something subtle and enduring is trying to be rediscovered and remembered and it seems to take some big trouble to awaken to it.

Modern cultures face long-term dangers of global warming and threats of global terrors that won't simply go away. The black dog of chaos has already pulled at the threads of existence. The design of life has already unraveled enough that the young grow up amidst great uncertainty about the future of the world, while the old have a tendency to forget who they are. The threads of life lie tangled and confused upon the ground as if waiting for initiatory events in which both young and old take up the threads and help to weave the whole thing again.

In facing the sense that the ends of time have come around again, both the young and the old may find new connections to the threads of the eternal that wind through each life and thread it to the Soul of the World. When times become dark with uncertainty both old roots and new shoots are needed for holding the endings and beginnings together.

CHAPTER 4

THE RIGHT TROUBLE

The Old Woman who weaves the world tries continually to make it all as beautiful as it can be. Yet she can never complete the task. Always some trouble, some darkness or distortion, some irregularity or imperfection gets in the way. Even though most people try to avoid trouble and many aspire to perfection, in the end what troubles us the most keeps the world going.

It turns out that the world can only end if everything becomes perfect. In the equation of creation and destruction, adding the final touch can be the kiss of death. Perfection is connected to death. To make perfect means "to bring to completion," "to make fully," "to go all the way through the form and complete it," "to finish it off," de facto, the End.

The imperfections of the world keep the whole impossible enterprise from reaching the point of completion. The impossible tasks, the broken hearts, and utter failures actually sustain the world; while everything perfectly finished soon passes away, too complete for this troublesome, imperfect realm.

Everything on earth involves the imperfect weaving together of eternity with all that is temporary, limited, incomplete, and of the moment. So the storyteller breaks a story at the end, the master potter leaves a spot unglazed, the Old Woman of the World leaves a loose thread for the black dog of chaos to pull upon. In this life there is no perfect bargain, no complete deal, no free lunch. In the long run, it is not fitting that everything should fit just so.

None of us would be here if things had worked out perfectly at any time before. This world and each person in it remains unfinished; remains because of being incomplete and unresolved. In this world, especially when things rattle and become uncertain, it's best to be an "imperfectionist."

THE PERFECT MATE

Those who sell schemes for the perfect life are not living the lives they were given. Those who seek perfection fear to face the odd designs already woven within them. People try to appear perfect, yet whatever becomes "perfection" has no need for anything else. Those who insist on finding the perfect match often wind up alone and empty-handed. Death is the only perfect match, the only real completion found in this life.

A genuine life requires some clumsiness just as love requires true vulnerability. In this world full of longing and seeking, only a broken heart can open wide enough for the "love dogs" to enter. When people fall in love they fall for what is broken or wounded, strange or incomplete in each other. Beauty is not only more than skin deep; beauty has something odd, unusual, unexpected, and unfinished about it.

Seeking perfection not only leads to disappointment, it also causes people to miss their real appointments with fate and with destiny. Those who look for the perfect spouse always find themselves deeply disappointed. Still, the idea of perfection seduces many. It's like the man who was complaining to everyone that he was lonely and had no one to love. A friend asked if he had tried this or that approach. He said he had tried everything a person could try.

He had gone far out in the world seeking the "perfect woman," but try as he might he couldn't find her. Each time he met someone with attractive qualities he also found some flaw that troubled him. No matter the depth of the positive traits, each little flaw would grow bigger before his evaluating eye.

Finally, he met a woman who seemed perfect in all regards; she had no flaws and he was completely enthralled with her. The friend asked, "Why then all this loneliness and constant complaining?" "Well, it turned out that she too was looking for the perfect mate," said the dejected and disappointed man.

People fall in love because the imperfections in each allow them to fit together. Love, which often provides the most perfect and complete moments on this earth, must be made from the imperfections of the lovers. Perfection means completion, yet love is always beginning, always ready to forgive and to start the whole thing over again. That's why lovers speak of forever and until the end of time.

Those who love know that there is no end of time, just as there can be no end to the ways of loving. Those who love life learn that the ends of time are threaded to the roots of eternity; that learning what to love in this world and how to love being in it opens life to the presence of eternal things that assist all of life to continue.

Those who insist on perfection in this realm have not truly begun to live here. Like the man seeking perfection in others, they haven't learned to accept their own flaws. All loving begins in the lover and extends from there. Loving others depends upon finding love in oneself. Loneliness involves an inability to be with oneself. Forgiveness of one's own flaws may be required if a person would fully connect to the imperfect realm of earthly existence.

THEORY OF TROUBLE

Sometimes it's better to learn from the nature of the trouble we find ourselves in. The perfectionist required qualities in others that he couldn't find in himself. In the end, those who seek perfection cause a great deal of trouble. They want everything to be just right and that makes most things seem quite wrong. Those who would fix everything and get things just right often cause the most trouble for everyone else.

People try to teach the young to avoid errors, yet the best opportunities for learning occur after mistakes have been made. Teaching begins where trouble raises important issues of life, so does learning. The desire to learn awakens where people lack knowledge and make mistakes.

Learning to sail involves encounters with rough weather and getting wet. Unless the deep waters are entered the sailor's skills remain untested. "Smooth seas make bad sailors," people used to say. For, this life has a sink or swim quality. Hints of fate and destiny trouble the soul from within and stir the psychic waters throughout life. Those who avoid the storms also avoid learning how they are intended to swim in this life. In trying to avoid mistakes, people make a serious mistake.

People "find themselves" when in some kind of trouble. What troubles us always seems bigger than we are, it grabs hold of us and we find ourselves being pulled deeper and deeper into it. That's the point of trouble: to get us into deeper waters than we might choose on our own. People have problems and can even handle them, but people "find themselves" when in the midst of what truly troubles them.

Real trouble has purpose hidden in it; that's why it's so troubling to us. Typically, serious trouble must develop for us to recall what is most important to us. For what truly troubles us would also change us. Trouble wants us to face up to it; to turn and face what we came here to learn about. The right trouble draws on all our resources, making us more resourceful and more aware of capacities we didn't know were there. The right trouble can make us more resilient, more creative, and less troubled in general.

Those who would avoid trouble at all costs simply wind up in the wrong trouble. In the end everyone gets into some kind of trouble, but wisdom depends on being in the right trouble. Being wise doesn't keep us completely out of trouble, but leads us to finding the right trouble to be in. That's a message from the black dog: find the right trouble and learn from it who you already are.

THE GIFT HORSE

It's like the old man who had an eye for trouble and saw the world differently from his neighbors. He lived simply and quietly with his family in the foothills of life. After a long day working in the fields, he looked over his little herd of horses and discovered that one of his mares had disappeared. His family and neighbors helped search the surrounding area, but when night fell the mare was nowhere to be found.

Eventually, everyone gave up the search. They were good neighbors and all offered condolences to the old man, "We are sorry that this unfortunate incident has happened to you and added trouble to your life." The old man remarked, "The loss of the mare is not necessarily a bad thing. Simply because we cannot see the unseen causes, it doesn't mean that all is lost. The true worth of things only appears over time."

The next morning, the old man saw two horses coming towards his house. He recognized the mare that had run off and soon could see that a fine stallion followed where she led. Even from a distance, he could tell that the mighty stallion was a war horse of great stature and important value. Later, he inquired throughout the area whether anyone had reported the loss of such a fine horse. The local official advised him to keep the stallion until someone reported it missing.

That evening, the old man's family and neighbors celebrated the return of the mare and the arrival of the great stallion. At the celebration, he was called upon to make a speech to mark the surprising increase in fortune. The old man remarked calmly, "The acquisition of the stallion is not necessarily a good thing. Life is full of surprises; one thing quickly turns into another. The true worth of something only appears as the whole story unfolds."

A week later, the old man's son took the stallion out for a ride. Not being skilled in handling such a great horse, the boy made a mistake and suffered a terrible fall. As a result, his leg was badly broken. The family and neighbors crowded around the boy and commented, "This is an awful thing that has happened. That strange stallion has brought bad luck to the whole family." The old man stood by the boy and observed, "An accident is not simply accidental; even a wound is not necessarily a bad thing. The true worth of things cannot be found on the surface of life."

Some time later that country became embroiled in a cruel and unjust war. All the youth of the kingdom were called to serve in the army. Although the enterprise was clearly founded upon narrow interests and false pretenses, many answered the call and willingly entered the battle. The old man's neighbors lamented heavily as they watched their children enter the mindless fields of war.

To ensure that no one could escape the battle, military officers went from house to house in search of any who could fight. Inevitably, they came upon the old man's compound. Seeing the great stallion in the yard, they considered, "This must be the home of a great warrior. But why has this coward not gone off to war?" They searched the entire property but could find only the old man, his elderly wife and their crippled son. The officers concluded, "This young man would have been a fine soldier if it were not for his wounded leg. We cannot take him in this condition."

Thus, the wounded son was exempted from fighting in the disastrous war. As reports of massive deaths arrived from the latest battle front, the neighbors reconsidered the entire course of events. With amazement they declared, "What wisdom that old man has, he can foresee good where others see only trouble and he can spot the shadow where most see only immediate benefits!"

Wisdom, they used to say, combines insight with experience and vision with maturity. If maturity expands one's vision it leads to wisdom; if not, maturity becomes simple degeneration. The old man had learned to observe trouble and see what was trying to occur behind the obvious facts. Trouble is the persistent turbulence between a person and his fate. How often does real trouble bring out the hidden qualities inside people.

It's not to say that everything comes out fine in the end; as in the story, people die all the time. There are plenty of false leaders and people keep volunteering for the wrong battles. Only those who have yet to learn the ways of this world and the sorrow it can cause celebrate war and conflict. How often does a victory turn out to be hollow? Then again, how frequently does an injury indicate where something necessary might be learned?

When in the right trouble we awaken to inner resources and draw upon what is second nature to us. When the common solutions fail to help, we learn that we are carried by patterns beyond our usual awareness, by portions of eternity buried within from the very beginning. Trouble turns our lives upside down, but also inside out; so that the inclinations of the soul can be seen and known.

Our real troubles stem from twists of fate and mysteries that intrigue the soul. Mystery is what trouble is aimed at; some intriguing mystery hides behind all the troubles we find ourselves in. People get into all kinds of trouble in order to find the right trouble and thereby the right way for them to go in life.

The right trouble releases what fate has in store for us; for hints of destiny emerge exactly from the twists of fate. The son of that old man had destiny beyond the foolish war; his broken, twisted leg kept him from succumbing to the wrong fate. Fate is the twist in the story, the necessary turn of events that turns each of us towards our destiny. Finding the ways that the soul genuinely fits into life is worth all the trouble in the world

Black dogs, dark horses, broken hearts, this world is made of troubles that won't leave us alone until we find the unseen thread that tries to pull us secretly from within. Only when the story has been lived out can we tell which was the right trouble and which the wrong battle to be in. The black dog is the inner limp we can't fully disguise, the loss that remains with us, the tragedy that won't release us, the dark edge that shades all real knowing. The black dog is the trouble that people find themselves in when they finally find themselves.

NECESSITY

The Old Woman doesn't trouble too much over all the mess; she has seen it all before, the wars and rigged elections, the grandiose ideas and the mean-spirited plots. Did you think she didn't know the Black Dog was there? Did you think she forgot him each time she wandered over to stir the soup of necessity? The Old Woman knows that the hound of chaos will undo all life's beautiful designs whenever things get too close to perfection.

She knows that chaos shadows all of creation. After all, it's her cave, her soup, her dog. She weaves with the worn fingers of time but has the touch of eternity. She's been there all along, behind the scenes, spinning and winding and recycling the threads of existence. The Old Woman is the original recycler. She knows all the cycles of existence and knows when it's time to recycle things again.

The Old Woman tolerates all the messes that people make, all the collapsed projects, the fallen empires and the unfinished business. She doesn't mind because she intends to weave it all again. She loves the making, the shaping of the design, the weaving together of diverse threads, even the biting down necessary to quicken the seeds of life.

The old Greeks called her Ananke or Necessity. All the gods had to bow to her, out of necessity. For necessity wasn't simply the mother of invention, but was also the mother of time, the dame of fortune and the Mistress of Fate who reweaves life from all mistakes and endings and from the great mess in the middle. In this world, creation and destruction are both parts of Necessity. It's messy and confusing; irrational, confounding, and upsetting, tragic and comic, full of anguish and loss. But it's all necessary.

Being fully alive and taking part while things fall apart means becoming more like the Old Woman, more connected to the oldness in the world, more willing to touch the threadbare bones of existence and wait for new designs to appear. And, more aware that some thing must be attended to out of sheer necessity. The willingness to accept that things have become undone helps things to begin again. Such humility and acceptance is troubling for those who only champion progress or insist upon superiority and endless growth. Yet in the dark times, recycling and reweaving, remembering and re-creating become more valuable than simplistic beliefs in perfection, endless progress and pointless growth.

As in so many tales, the shift from destruction to creation happens at the last minute, in the last possible moment. That moment opens up as the psyche begins to accept the mess of life and look for second chances. The gifts of survival and access to ancient resources come at the edge of what we know; in the midst of the mess, when all seems lost. Right at the end, things try to turn around and begin again. In preparing the last rites, we find the touch of eternity and the lasting threads necessary for life to continue; for that reversal is necessary as well.

There are times when it's better to let sleeping dogs lie and other times when you might as well kick the big dog. For what truly troubles us will not leave us alone; it dogs our steps and shades our door. In the black dog times everyone is in trouble and it's better to go looking for the right trouble before the wrong trouble finds you unawares.

In the black dog times there's more than enough trouble to go around. No matter where you turn in nature or in culture there's necessary work to do. It isn't simply that the garments of culture have worn thin, exposing everyone to the raw greed of materialists and the fanaticism of fundamentalists. It's as if humanity has broken a secret bond with the world of Nature and become estranged from "inner nature" as well.

Long before people began to blindly drill and drain resources from the earth, human cultures had lost proper connections to the hidden sources of life. The blind exploitation of the earth follows upon broken connections to the realm of nature and dissociation from the delicate connections to the divine aspects of this world. Mass cultures diminish the value of individual lives and the rise of literalism replaces the great mystery of being alive with the dull history of simply surviving.

Besides the ecological disasters and the cultural crises there is a deepening crisis of meaning, a loss of meaning in the course of life. Eternity has become too big to imagine and the instinctive sense of wonder proper to viewing the world has been replaced with dutiful creeds and blind ideologies. The sense of impending doom also grows from a loss of living imagination and the increasing sense that it's all an accident, accidental lives, meaningless death, a pointless existence in an accidental universe.

Sometimes things have to begin at the very end. Sometimes facing the end is the only way to begin again. For the end turns out to have less to do with closure than with a certain closeness to the places of origin, a feeling for touching the invisible roots of life, a sense of being near the source, the way it was back at the very beginning, once upon a time.

In the beginning there was "The Word" and "The End" is supposed to be the final word. Yet The End turns out to be more than that, for the word end refers to "that which is left," to what's left at the end, after it's all over. In this imperfect world there is always a loose end, a tail end or a remnant; always some residue that simply remains. In the end there is no end, for something always remains and everything begins again from the leftovers and the remainders of all that went before. No matter what people claim to know or wish to believe, no one ever finds the exact beginning and the final end never comes.

Beginnings and endings come and go, both trailing with roots of eternity. For end and beginning are both mythic terms and anything mythical comes laden with many meanings. In the end there is always something left, always some aftermath, always more "second chances," always some unfinished business and loose ends that can't be neatly tied up. From what went on before, things go on again. In the end, there is no real end in sight.

This world has always been about to end; it has always been hanging by a thread; but that thread connects to the eternal realm, to the world behind the world. Like the beginning, the end is a threshold where eternity exchanges with time. When all seems torn to shreds and about to collapse, eternity can be found hiding just in the nick of time, in the places where time breaks open and the eternal enters again. What we call "The End" is a crossing place where some things conclude while something else continues on.

Ever since the beginning of time, the world has been about to end. The fear that the world will end entirely misses the point, for the world survives even the stories about the end of the world. The End is always near, yet hard to reach. In The End there is no end, for the ends of time are near the roots of eternity and the ends of the earth secretly touch the eternal world behind the world.

Certainly disasters happen all over the place and catastrophes occur everywhere. Villainy often triumphs and chaos frequently rules. Mighty civilizations fall; grand ideas wear thin, wide-flung forests become barren desert sands. The world comes to many ends; it ends all the time. The world collapses and comes to ruin in many ways, but it doesn't simply end. Rather, in reaching the end again, it keeps returning to the beginning, like a favorite story. Beginning and end each give birth to the other, like night and day.

When people feel The End fast approaching, the beginning is also close at hand. The world, ever on the verge of explosion or collapse is also an eternal drama, a story being told from beginning to end, again and again. At the "end of the world as we know it" the Unseen World waits to be found again. The "ends of the earth" secretly touch the subtle ground of the Otherworld, the hidden and indelible source of all that appears as reality in this world. In the end it is the connection with eternal things that must be found again.

Eternity is the bottom line of time and the hidden source of all that takes place in this world where time is the troubled child of eternity and night. The world goes on because of hidden continuities, because it is continuous and contiguous with the Unseen, secretly tied to the Otherworld, the dwelling place of the divine. The problem isn't that soon it will all come to an end, rather the issue is how to act when it seems that way.

At the end of the rope of science and sociology, at the conclusion of the "age of history," the fine filaments of mythic imagination try to slip back into awareness. Sometimes, the very ground beneath our feet must feel threatened before the subtle earth of living imagination can be found again. Sometimes, we have to approach The End before the subtle, mostly unseen levels of life become approachable again.

II

Living at the Ends of Time

CHAPTER 5

LIVING AT THE ENDS OF TIME

In ancient world views the daily world of time and space was seen as a limited manifestation of the World Behind the World. The world behind and beyond the common realm was considered to be the "Real behind the real." Anything that appeared in reality had first to arise from the world of abundance, the eternal and enduring realm behind everything found "in reality."

The modern world has lost the innate sense of connection to the Real and thereby to the realm of abundance behind and beyond the daily world. In losing the immediate sense of the divine behind all designs the sense of life's innate abundance has disappeared to be replaced by what people call the "real world." In losing the felt sense that abundant and meaningful things dwell nearby the sense of meaning in this world has been steadily diminishing.

To be modern has come to mean to be lost, to be losing time all the time and to be running out of space as overpopulation overwhelms even the most private places. Faced with the disappearance of species, the decimation of great forests, and the melting of protective ice caps, it becomes easy to feel that all will soon be lost.

To be modern means to feel the world wasting away as natural resources are wantonly wasted day after day and the number of wasted lives and wasted deaths grows amidst religious fervors and overheated political issues. Rents in the tissues of nature are paralleled by the shredding of sense and meaning in culture as the two great garments of the world become increasingly torn and worn.

It isn't simply that people feel a loss of time, but also that it is a time of loss. There is a loss of sense as in the sense of direction, the sense of purpose, the sense of meaning.

Holes in the ozone layers expose people to damaging solar rays and severe climate changes while floods of change sweep through social systems and institutions emptying them of former meanings and washing away the stability they are intended to provide. To be alive at this point in time means to be consciously exposed to the raw forces of nature and the rough edges of culture.

To be modern means to be in a great hurry, careening towards an uncertain future and increasingly dislodged from the past. Human events become trapped at the soul-starved surface of life where brief flashes of fame become a substitute for struggling to live the dreams inherent in one's soul. Narrow forms of egotism pass for accomplishment and cleverness takes the place of genuine learning and the search for real knowledge.

There is a growing insensitivity to inauthentic things and a decreasing aptitude for what might be genuine. The instinct for finding meaning becomes replaced with a "concentration of cunning" that trades only in short-term gains while a sea of despair grows just under the flashy, rushing surface of modern life.

Things move faster and faster as the elements of time become smaller and smaller, each digital bit flashing from a myriad of clocks seemingly timed to the final countdown. Life becomes reduced to fractions of time, endless details, and mindless trivia. Yet all the deconstructed bits and bytes can never be added back up to produce meaning or restore what has already been lost. For it is the whole thing, the sense of wholeness, and the meaning of things that has gone missing.

Amidst a mania for measuring and counting people collect reams of statistics and compile endless opinion polls as if to arrive at something meaningful and enduring by piling up facts and figures. The frenzy of counting is secretly connected to the sense that the end is near and everything must be accounted for.

Yet no amount of counting or accounting can add back the missing sense of wholeness. For intimations of wholeness require the touch of the eternal. Wholeness must be intuited and sensed and found in open moments when the march of time is interrupted, when time stands still and the "glue of the world" returns and holds everything together for just a moment.

The glue of imagination that secretly connects the elements of the world has diminished with the increasing separation between subject and objects. The subtle sense of Eros requires slow motions and intimate touching, not high-speed connections; the intimacy of genuine knowledge depends upon quiet reflection not rapid reproduction. Part of what has been lost in the reckless rushing of modernity is the sense that each life has an authentic interior that shelters important emotions and inherent purpose; that the dignity of existence includes a necessary instinct to find beauty and encounter meaning.

While many people fear a sudden and devastating end about to come, there is a "slow apocalypse" characterized by a loss of life throughout the course of life, a draining of life from the ages and stages of human existence. In fearing that The End is coming soon, people miss the sense that it's already here in the loss of life that people feel each day. In the end, The End may come as a lessening of life rather than a grand and fiery finale.

LESS AND LESS

At the beginning of things and near the end facts and myth approach each other. That old idea came to mind when I heard that someone at the United Nations had gathered reports from people all over the world about what troubled them most in their local communities. The report was summarized at an international gathering that brought together youth from many parts of the world. By the time the litany of world troubles had been recited tears streamed down the faces of the young people. A great sadness filled the room as the worldwide sense of loss became palpable.

The report of world troubles was compelling in the way that an accident compels people to consider the frailty of life, and like a tragic accident it stopped all other conversations. I am still struck by that occasion and the courage with which the young people faced up to the agonies of the world around them and asked pertinent questions. Despite the growing presence of tragedy and loss in the room, they preferred to know the situation in the world around them. They seemed to find each other more valuable and necessary as they considered the conditions to which they had been born.

The report was the kind of thing made possible by the exaggerations of modern technology, yet it had a fairy-tale quality as well. People at the UN invited reports of all the issues that currently bite at the hearts and souls of humanity and eat away at the tissues of hope. On one level it seemed but one more accumulation of blind data to be placed in some corner of the Age of Information. As if in the mania for collecting details someone was bound to harvest the facts of human suffering, digitally digest them, and reduce it all to a database.

Yet sometimes a document says more than it intends to say; sometimes the facts reveal more than anticipated, sometimes a deeper truth slips through a methodical report. The notion of collecting the troubles of the world had the sense of a reverse Pandora's Box and something mythic slipped into the project. The idea had a story-like quality as in fairy tales when the ruler becomes uneasy about his subjects and desires to know what troubles the realm. Soon messengers scurry in all directions. Eventually, someone has to guess the name of a dwarf or it turns out that the princess won't marry unless someone decodes the source of the ailment that troubles her heart.

Naming the trouble correctly can help to break the spells that stop the genuine flow of life and help people return to living in meaningful ways.

This UN report certainly named some troubles; it captured a dark picture of the earthly realm and the increasing struggles of the human souls that dwell within it.

A simple question was put: What torments and troubles the common folks in each part of the world? Regular people were given the opportunity to describe what felt most wrong with their lives, with their villages, their tribes, their cities, their governments, their religions, and even their leaders. Questionnaires went into circulation in many languages and the accumulation of sufferings and woes began to gather.

Every kind of threat, disaster, and disorder appeared and each was fed into collecting points. Soon a river of anguish and pain written in all the tongues of the earth began to flow towards the United Nations. Naming all the problems of the diverse peoples of the earth created a kind of temple of troubles. Inside that temple there was a tabernacle of emptiness; for what echoed most loudly from so many different tongues was the shared sense of loss that seemed to be growing in all the corners and cultures throughout the world.

Tragedy, loss, and disorientation were common threads in the multilingual answers that whispered of a deepening sense of despair common to the peoples of the earth. Regardless of standards of living, people of all kinds felt a loss with regard to the essential qualities of life. Some acutely felt the loss of a common past and the stability once provided by traditions. Others saw the future disappearing before their eyes as a result of reckless exploitation and subsequent natural disasters. The litany of loss had begun and the tidal wave of human grief and suffering threatened to drown everyone unless the torrent could somehow be organized and shaped into tributaries of trouble.

Most things can be organized into four parts. There are the four corners of the world and the four directions. Four sides can make a house or else can shape a prison. There are the four chambers of the human heart, the four gospels, the "four noble truths." Even The End announces itself with the four horsemen of the apocalypse. Dividing something in four tends to give it a sense of order and completion.

People have long had the habit of organizing by fours and soon enough the anguish of humanity was divided into four areas of suffering common to all peoples: cultural issues, political problems, economic stresses, and environmental disasters. The United Nations report on all the troubles of all the people in the world would be organized into four categories that reflect essential areas of human society and human concerns. Each category would then be cooked down to a brief description, then each would be condensed to a single, symbolic word.

First gather the impossible list of all the troubles in the world; next, make a stew of the worldwide lament; then render the whole thing down to a few words… that's fairy-tale stuff. That's not just a report of epic proportions, but a tale of mythic inclinations.

THE CULTURAL MESS

The realm of cultural troubles included the loss of tribal and regional languages and the imposition of modern speech and forms of mass communication. It seems that cultures all over the world are in danger of losing the traditions and styles that make them unique and distinguished. Older folks can't keep up with the latest technological gadgets and find themselves with fewer and fewer positions of respect to aspire to. Young people can communicate rapidly from all over the earth, yet often have little of meaning to say.

With less and less to pass along to their children, the human instinct and need to leave a living legacy becomes frustrated and denied. In losing connections to the past, people sense the future slipping away as well. An absence of true elders and the increasing violence of youth seemed to bespeak a great unraveling in undeveloped, developing, and overdeveloped cultures throughout the world. People everywhere seem to feel a loss of meaningful rites and practices that could ease the burdens of living and create experiences of social unity and cultural coherence.

Ethnic cleansing and religious intolerance seem to grow along with the increase in human populations. In some areas religious groups suffer persecution by oppressive and tyrannical regimes. In other areas religious dogmas and beliefs become the source of terror and oppression. Harsh religious practices and inhumane rules replace the sense of institutions intended to protect people and promote a unity of concerns. A storm of despair was clearly gathering and stirring both the waters of depression and the fires of terrorism.

Meanwhile, hordes of people become refugees, uprooted by the violence of wars, driven by the ravages of drought and famine. More and more people feel homeless and out of place. Despite the virtual sense of a "global village," there is a growing sense of global homelessness. The cultural woes were gathered into a summary of loss and disorientation, oppression and homelessness. There was an increasing sense of people feeling uprooted and ungrounded, alienated in their own lands and considered illegal aliens in other lands. The people of the earth are feeling more and more homeless. When rendered down to a single word, more and more people feel "rootless" in this world disoriented by speed and radical change.

POLITICAL PROBLEMS

Political issues are ubiquitous; political problems began at the founding of the first town. *Polis* is the Greek word for city or town. Gather enough people and the dramas of power and position are bound to begin. Inevitably people take opposing views of common issues. Soon, major parties form; then "splinter groups" appear and sharply conflicting ideologies develop. As conflicts intensify near neighbors become vilified, exiled, tortured, scapegoated, and cast into the wilderness. Politics includes both the instinct to unite with others and the conflicts that gathering together generates.

Modern politics involves an increasing alienation amongst people as ever greater disparities grow between those who have more than they know what to do with and those who don't have half of what they need. People feel increasingly unheard while being herded along by blind systems that benefit only an elite class. More and more people feel lost amidst issues and systems that they cannot affect or even understand. Amidst high-speed communications, rapid transport and digital technology, most people feel less able to do anything about social conditions and political problems in their own towns.

Increasingly alienated by technocracies, people feel trapped in abstract procedures that do not lead to dignity in daily life or provide hope for the future. As the "art of politics" devolves into blind battles and raw conflicts of interest, people suffer a decline of civilization and a diminishing of the beauty in the world around them. Citizens in both overdeveloped and undeveloped countries watch the brutalities of life march across screens and monitors while feeling increasingly unable to stop the procession of tragedies.

From the appalling lists of political crimes, the bloody reports of brutal oppressions and mindless exploitations, the UN commission on the current state of the world tried to extract one word to characterize how people feel about local and international politics. Increasingly, the UN found, the people of the world feel "powerless."

ECONOMIC STRESS

Politics, they say, is always local and economics begins at home. Combining the Greek words "oiko" and "nomous" gives us economics. "Oiko" means house or home and "nomos" refers to one who manages. Economics involves the handling and management of the day-to-day affairs of house and home and by extension the trade and exchanges involving one's homeland. Economics is a catchword for the common commerce of people, the back and forth of all the basic needs as well as the collision of the common greeds found in human life.

In modern cultures the common issues of house and home become abstracted into principles of supply and demand, then acted out by transnational corporations feeding and misleading the citizens. In the worldwide marketplace of disposable products, human dignity and self-worth are also for sale and increasingly devalued and discounted. In the world-view in which time equals money, most people experience a loss of "quality time" and a diminishing of the meaning and value of local place.

The massing of mass societies leads to greater and greater gaps between the rich and the poor and the increasing disparities actually diminishes the dignity of all involved. The "consumer society" begins to consume itself as infantile greed and adolescent fantasies of wealth and power replace healthy notions of managing the home and respecting the homeland.

Under the "rule of scarcity" people believe that there's never enough to go around and that justifies the resolve that: "I'm going to get mine." Simplistic notions of winners and losers replace the subtle sense of the dignity of all life. Soon, the immature urges to power and maniacal devouring of resources become sanctified as raw greed becomes elevated to a virtue.

Under the banners of the free market and justice of the marketplace more and more people lose the freedom to choose how to live and the right to serve and preserve both local nature and local culture. Modern economics often functions as a secular religion, a fundamentalism based in fixed ideas and abstract laws that seem to justify worldwide pathologies of individual greed and collective consumption.

Rootless and powerless, the hungry souls of the world are met by a collective ruthlessness that seems to know no bounds. The report on economic troubles of the worldwide village of human suffering had to be boiled down to a bottom line and the word the report used to describe the prevailing economic attitudes and practices was: "ruthless."

ENVIRONMENTAL FEARS

Natural environments are severely affected by the practices of economics in modern cultures that generate a deep sense of alienation from the natural surroundings and dissociation from the earth itself. The earth, once the image of home and source of natural abundance, has been reduced to an aggregation of resources to fight over. The sense of earth as home, as dwelling of the ancestors, and mother to the future has been replaced with a sense of the earth as an economic object to be exploited for short-term gain and immediate power.

Reports from every corner of the globe detail how the earth has been recklessly mined, mindlessly drilled and pumped in order to extract resources to satisfy the two-headed dragon of greed and consumption. Unique areas of nature have been stripped and torn, rivers choked with pollution, forests clearcut and slashed, the skies etched and ulcerated by acids so that the glorious, pitiless sun glowers harshly on increasingly exposed children. Terrible viruses proliferate, cows go mad while sheep are cloned and the very seeds and grains of life are altered for short-term gain and delusions of controlling nature's fruits.

Even the unseen realm of atoms and nuclei becomes penetrated and polarized, exploited and exploded leaving clouds of confusion and waste that no one wants or knows what to do with. The threat of nuclear destruction competes with the sense of elemental collapse amidst a confusion of blind greed and dull ignorance about the nature of human nature and the importance of the earth as the ground of reality and resting place for the dreams of humanity.

As the report on world troubles focused upon the decimation of nature's intricate web of beauty, the sense of loss and disorientation intensified again. The wild separation of the practices of culture from the rhythms of nature leaves people in a desperate lurch facing a chasm of growing uncertainty. Amidst descriptions of the rapid growth of populations the world over there is also a growing fear that there might be no future generations. When the weight of the reports of environmental damage and exploitation of the earth was weighed and measured and fully faced, the word the report offered as best able to convey the sense of devastation felt throughout the world was "futureless."

Less and less, went the mantra of loss as the world seemed to be diminishing before the glazed eyes of humanity. Having cooked the woes of the world down to four desperate words, Rootless, Powerless, Ruthless and Futureless, the researchers of trouble decided to reduce the entire report to a single word that could sum up the conditions of the common person in the modern world. They sought for a quintessential word that could express the anguish and despair at the center of the increasing lament of the nations of the earth.

Needless to say, the word would have to end in "less," to be in keeping with the mantra of less and less and the diminishing of the world. Eventually, they settled on a word that seemed able to sit at the center of the temple of woes. In the midst of the emptying of the world and the unraveling of the fabrics of both culture and nature, the world and the course of individual life within it had become for most people "meaningless." One aching word spoken repeatedly in many languages and in different ways by the disparate voices of the nations of the world when asked to describe the conditions of life in the darkening times: meaningless.

Feeling increasingly rootless, homeless, powerless, and futureless, people feel the whole thing fast becoming meaningless; the whole thing meaning less and less. It's as if a new form of the Dark Ages has fallen upon the world as the Enlightenment recedes into the shadows. People sense the end of the world, not just because some lunatic playing with delusions of power might blow it all up, but because of a loss of home and of hope, a loss of roots and customs, of meaningful ideas and ideals and finally of meaning itself.

Like so many modern projects the initial step of gathering information and formulating the massive details had been quite effective. Yet, it became more clear that the problem wasn't that the troubles of the world were uncountable and untenable; rather that taken together they seemed so huge, so permeating and insurmountable. The trouble behind all the troubles was the seeming impossibility of the tasks required to change the hopeless direction of things, especially while feeling powerless to do so.

After the summary of the report had been given a great weight descended through the room, a heaviness that bordered on despair. It was not just that modern life has lost it's way, not simply that mass societies suffered with ideas of mass destruction, but the loss of the ancient sense of each life as meaningful and each death as significant. An increasing tension pits mass culture against the natural practice of becoming a genuine individual. The weight of mass culture can overwhelm the courage of the individual and leave them in despair.

Yet, we may loose hope in order to find a deeper sense of life only found after "all hope is lost." It is the nature of hope to become lost; what begins with high hopes often ends in deep despair. Any hope for this hopeless world might have to be found inside the currents of despair that increasingly accompany the news reports of cultural unraveling and environmental disasters.

Hope hid under the lid after Pandora's box opened, as if all the troubles of the world must be released and even cataloged before genuine hope can be found. Initial hopes tend to be false hopes and high hopes that never reach the ground of reality. After naïve hopes have been dashed against the hard edges of the world a second level of hope sometimes appears, a "hope against hope."

For, what can be found at the edge of hopelessness and in the depths of despair are the images hidden in the soul, the core imagination that waits to be found when all seems hopeless and the end is in sight. The second layer of hope includes a darker knowledge of the world and a sharper insight into one's own soul. Perhaps it would be better to name the hidden hope "imagination," for it is imagination that keeps the world a becoming thing.

The core and crucial power of humanity is not simple hope, rather it is the capacity for renewal that attends the inborn powers of imagination. Hope is reborn each time someone awakens to the genuine imagination of their own heart. Hope springs eternal as long as people can find a sense of mythic imagination that can create ways to hold the ends and beginnings together, even when things appear hopeless to most.

MYTHIC INOCULATION

Although decidedly frail, perpetually foolish, and seemingly about to destroy the whole thing, humans are blessed with an imagination equal to the world and essential to its ways of continuing. In the great drama of life the human soul becomes the makeweight, the extra quantity, and uniquely living quality needed to help tip the balance of the world towards continuing creation.

The *gravitas* of the awakened soul helps tie the thread of the eternal to the presence of the present moment. When the dark times come around and the end seems near again, it becomes more essential for the individual person to learn and live the story the soul carries from before birth. If people are not invited into a living stream of culture, tragedies begin to grow. Unlived dreams become tragedies waiting to happen. Lose the sense that each life carries meaning and death becomes meaningless as well.

Traditionally, it has been the function of myth to wrap people in stories that make intuitive sense of the world and point to meaningful ways of being part of it. Yet, under the harsh rule of materialism and the dull spell of literalism myth becomes dismissed as fantasy, as something out of touch with reality. Yet in the inner recesses of the human soul, where the facts of life mingle with the mysteries of eternity, myth means "emergent truth."

In the long run, and it is the long run that's of increasing concern, myth makes meaning. The job of myth is to make the world meaningful and hold everyone in the mythic imagination of the living story. Meaning is a storied thing and many meanings appear and can become clear once the storyline has been found. Each life, each myth has its own inner logic, its own subjective truth, its own persuasive beauty and its own dramatic form.

Myth makes meaning and helps reveal the significance of both inner and outer events. Troubled and threatened as it may be, the world remains a mystery trying to be revealed. Reality isn't fully real until its hidden meanings have been revealed. Every event, inner and outer, has hidden meaning waiting to be revealed. Yet, it takes a story, a narrative shape to uncover the meanings that hide within the facts of the matter.

Stories offer mythic contexts, psychic subtexts, and subtle backgrounds for viewing and interpreting the world around us and the inevitable dramas and tragedies that befall us. Two great dramas appear on the same stage: the endless story of the world and the ongoing struggle of each human soul to awaken to a sense of meaning within that tale. The great wide world and the individual soul, each threaded through with many endings and beginnings that keep the drama of life going in tragic and surprising, in compelling and intricate ways.

Myth makes sense by holding things in the rhythm of beginning, middle, and end and placing each person in the patterns and plots of the eternal drama. Mythic sense reveals the themes that secretly run all the way through an entire life, the hidden threads that can draw disparate pieces together and shape them to a coherent inner story.

Myth opens immediate feelings for the great wonders of spirit as well as for the intricate territories of the soul. Myth includes all the invisible aspects of life, the missing parts and the hidden themes, the epic qualities and emotional tenors and all the mute and musical tones that shape the inward ground of being.

Only nature, with its endless variations and dramatic orchestrations can compare with the stream of images and intimations that flow from the living waters of mythic imagination. The inheritance of mythic imagination is one of the deepest, most natural and pertinent powers of humankind. People are mythic by nature and instinctively imbued with nature's essential pattern of life, death, and renewal.

The real marketplace of humanity involves trading in surprising images and bold ideas, in genuine feelings of love, in bone-level feelings for justice and the presence of meaning waiting to be found both in the immediacy of the world and in the inner speculations of the soul. The human soul harbors an enduring power of imagination able to transcend both common sense and simple reality. Unlike fantasy that would escape from the pain of reality, imagination combines the concrete with the inspired. This deep sense of connecting to the spirit of life makes most sense when nothing else makes any sense.

At critical moments in history mythic sense tries to return to awareness in order to indicate life's inherent capacity for renewal. When the end seems near and nothing seems to make sense anymore, the sense of myth tries to return to make sense of all the endings and to hint at ways of beginning again. In the end there is no sense of closure, but a surprising mix of closings and openings, as the door of time swings loosely on the threshold of eternity. In the end, mythic sense returns bringing with it the wisdom of origins, the pulse of originality and the vitality of the unseen to the world-weary realm of literal reality.

Imagination connects a person to the divine aspects of the world, it adds the living element to the daily world and can alter reality in no time. As the poet said, "Eternity is in love with the productions of time."

So-called reality is the child of an ongoing love affair between time and eternity. Time begins in "all eternity" and returns there when it needs to be replenished. It only takes a little imagination to break the linear, literal spells of time and arrive back at the Once Upon a Time that is the origin of the soul to begin with.

Not just citizens of the world, not merely statistics without inherent meaning, humans are living metaphors, bodies and spirits conjoined with the glue of the soul and shaped by invisible threads of imagination and story. We cannot rescind this ancient and immediate heritage of imagination, for it is buried in the bones and laced into the body cell by cell. We are imaginative beings doused with eternity before our eyes ever opened upon this earth. From the beginning we see more than we can express and our last words fail to conclude the stories that live through us.

For we are lived through by energies, ideas and emotions that flow from the unseen world behind this world. We are overloaded by our own dreams, saddled with unusual fates and driven by unseen destinies. Were it not for the gravity that rests in our bones and vital organs, we would take flight. Were it not for the tangled relationships of past, present and future, we would escape every atmosphere and become the Unseen.

Despite the collapse of the immediacy of mystery into the confines of history, this down-to-earth world is also a mythic place, an ongoing production fashioned and staged by eternity. Despite the pressing problems and mounting concerns, the issue isn't so much saving the planet as saving humanity from itself again. When times become dark and difficult the issue for those on earth comes down to living authentically, to authenticating the purpose and meaning already present in each soul.

No solitary idea, no matter how great, no single notion or shared belief can shift the weight of the world towards a meaningful future; but the accumulated vitality of many lives lived more fully might become a meaningful makeweight in the balance between time and eternity. Strange as it may seem, individual consciousness forms the makeweight, and living out the hidden meanings within life helps to balance the weight of the world. Each living being wrapped around an invisible, eternal thread, each a story breaking out of the wall of time to sing its own unfinished song.

Life always hangs by a thread as all of time is loosely stitched on the "loom of eternity." The great hubris of all of life, the terrible and grand gestures of death, all played out again and again in the seas of time, pulled on by an imperishable tide. What we call the world is a reckless story, a wild, star-crossed narration being told through the breathing green garment of Nature and revealing itself in the tragedies and comedies of earthly life. The world is made of stories and cannot end unless all the tales reach the same conclusion. In the end there are too many plot twists to predict and too many loose threads to tie up. From some loose end or ragged remnant the whole tale begins again.

In mythic terms the issue isn't simply the end of the planet, but the further loss of the earth as a magical, mythical, imaginal realm. The issue is the growing poverty of imagination, the wound of separation from the subtle levels of life, the loss of tender connections to unseen things and the felt sense for the presence of beauty. The loss of the soul connection leaves humans in the lurch, falling out into a sullen void that avoids both the healing touch of genuine culture and the enlivening spirit of the natural world.

Myth means finding enough story to keep "re-storing" and "re-storying" the world. Whenever the end seems near it is important to have a mythic sense, a story-mind, an awareness of imaginal things, not simply a fantasy to escape with, but a sense of mythic imagination that can hold the ends and beginnings together.

Genuine stories can release us from the preoccupations of historical time and project us through the paradoxical present into Great Time. Myth implies a breach in the world, a rend in the dull continuity of the daily world that can generate life and open a Way or a Path to follow. Myth has a redeeming function that saves us from the blind pressures of time. Simply listening to a myth can release a person from the profane condition and the historical situation. Myth offers an inoculation against cynicism and the nihilism that grows where the threads of meaning have been lost.

Eternity waits at the edge of each day and hides until the last minute, only appearing in the "nick of time." The nick of time was once a notch on a stick used to measure the passing of loosely measured moments. Yet each nick is also a tear in the relentless rush of time, an opening that breaks time and stops the march of mortality allowing eternity to pour through the crack. Stories often depend upon the nick of time to ransom life from the edge of annihilation again.

CHAPTER 6

THE NET OF STORIES AND THE SWORD OF DOOM

Remember Scheherazade, who faced death with nothing to save her but stories? Her name means "born of a noble race" and she was known for her knowledge of ancient practices and old ideas. She had studied all the arts and sciences and collected enough books to constitute a great library. The woman who would come to be known the world over for *The Thousand and One Arabian Nights* was first known for her collection of a thousand and one books and her study of the nobility of the human soul.

"A thousand and one" is a mythical number; it means as many as you can count—plus one more. The additional one shifts things from the literal quantity to a mythical quality. Scheherazade was all about mythic things; she was a collector of timeless tales and a disciple of stories. It was that knowledge that enabled her to see what was wrong with the realm and the current regime. It was that practice that caused her to willingly face the end and risk her life at the edge of a sacrificial sword.

The story used to be widely known: how a young sultan was betrayed in love by his queen; how he became unbalanced and took revenge by sleeping each night with a maiden only to have her slain at the dawn of the following day. Each night crowned a new queen in that troubled realm and each day dawned with the death of love, with a loss of life, and a blind sacrifice of young womanhood.

As in a war that deprives a country of its sons, the madness of the king was draining the land of its innocent daughters. Because the ruler felt betrayed by life, he felt justified in betraying the lives of others. A "little death" had occurred in the heart of that king and he had fallen out of the story of life. It's the kind of thing that can happen to any who try their hand at love. When it happens to those who have the power of life and death in their hands it is usually others who suffer the fatal consequences. As is the case to this day, a wounded ruler soon damages the lives of the common people.

The wound of the king fell like a blade through the heart of the kingdom as each day arrived with the Vizier bringing the sword of doom to the neck of a maiden who had been queen for a single night. Scheherazade was the daughter of that Vizier and she observed the increasing darkness in her father's spirit. One day she asked him what caused his tragic mood and why depression and despair seemed to spread throughout the realm. The old man refused to answer. He claimed that great dangers would result from revealing state secrets. He said that the security of the country would be compromised.

In order to drive the point home, he told an old folktale about a wife who endangered her husband's life by asking that everything secret be revealed to her. By causing him to tell secrets she placed him in mortal danger. The lesson of the story was supposed to close the book on the discussion of secrets. But Scheherazade knew that there were two kinds of secrets held in the human heart. She knew that some secrets were sublime; they were carried for life and for the sake of life. She also knew that some secrets became the death of the soul if they were not brought out and exposed to the light of day.

Scheherazade knew the difference between secrets and she knew that the secrets held by the Vizier and the king were causing the entire realm to become fearful and sick. Besides that, she reminded her father, she was a daughter, not a wife, and mistress of her own fate. The tale he had chosen missed the point altogether. She insisted upon knowing the real situation and the old man sorrowfully confessed the entire tragedy that ate away at the realm and brought death to the door of life at the dawning of each day.

Scheherazade volunteered to be the next queen and bride of death. She told her father to inform the king of her decision to offer herself despite the threat of death. The Vizier argued vehemently, but to no avail. If he wouldn't do his duty as counselor, she would report his failure to the king and offer herself anyway. Either she would be the cause of deliverance of the daughters of the Muslims or she would perish along with them.

What others ran away from Scheherazade willingly walked towards. It wasn't that she was tired of this world or numb to its pleasures and promises. It wasn't that she sought to sacrifice herself in order to arrive at heaven's gate in some martyred shape. Rather, she agreed to face death because of something she knew about life. Scheherazade was a student of stories; she knew that sometimes the only way to begin again was to face the end.

Scheherazade was prepared to face the sword of fate armed only with her own wits and the poetry of ancient stories. She would face the madness of the times with the weapons of timelessness. She requested that her sister Dunyazad accompany her on the fateful journey and outlined her strategy for their survival. Once in the company of the king, the younger sister was to ask for a story, saying that she loved her sister's stories and remarking how a good tale always helps to pass the time and ease the burdens of the soul. After that everything would be in the hands of the storyteller and the fates.

At the appointed time the two sisters presented themselves at the palace. The king was restless and willing enough to be distracted by a tale as they sat between the circling stars of the night and the blood-red promise of dawn. As the sultan reclined, Scheherazade began the strange tale of a merchant who unwittingly kills the son of a genie. Genies (or "djinns") were spirits or demons that dwelt between this world and the otherworld. They were part of the unseen, the "invisibles" that were there but not there.

They filled the spaces between more visible things and could appear as powerful or else be delicate. They were helpful or harmful depending on the conditions of the moment.

In this case, the merchant had eaten some dates and simply threw the seeds away. The genie's son was nearby sleeping inside his invisibility when the ill fated seeds struck him and killed him right off. The angry genie immediately knew that something had happened and arrived with a great sword his hands. He condemned the merchant to death, but agreed to postpone the sentence for one year so the merchant could take leave of his daughters and settle his affairs. The merchant sorrowfully accepted his painful fate and turned to put his earthly affairs in final order.

On the anniversary of the event with the dates, the merchant was returning to face his fate when he encountered three old men. Each of the old fellows was blind and each was being followed by strange-appearing animals. They made an odd impression and a compelling sight. When the merchant told the tale of what had befallen him with the son of the genie the blind men felt the situation to be unjust and offered to intercede on his behalf with the genie.

They traveled along together and when they came into the presence of the genie, each of the blind men bargained for a portion of the merchant's life. Each would offer the tale of how he came to be blind and was followed everywhere by his animals. If the genie found the stories to be vehicles of wonder, he would relinquish a third part of the merchant's life-blood in exchange for each tale. The genie couldn't resist his curiosity about the strange procession of blind men with their spellbound animals. The deal of exchanging tales of fate for life blood was struck on the spot and the genie's demand for vengeance was forestalled as the storytelling of the blind men commenced.

Scheherazade wove the strange details of the blind men's tales before the eyes of the troubled king. He became just as enthralled and curious as the vengeful genie. Suffice it to say that each story involved love and betrayal and that the animals following behind the blind men were embodiments of the anguished conditions the men carried in their hearts. Each tale revealed more of the sense of betrayal that permeates this world of beauty and sorrow. Each tale told moved closer to the condition that troubled the heart of the young sultan.

The story of the third blind man actually involved an unfaithful wife who now followed his every step, spellbound in the form of a mule. The young king followed every detail with fixed attention and was thoroughly shocked when Scheherazade stopped the story and stubbornly refused to take it another step further. The light of dawn was beginning to threaten the kingdom of the night and the storyteller offered the king a choice similar to that given to the vengeful genie.

Either he could raise the sword of death over her head or he could suspend the sentence for a day and a night and learn more of the fate of the merchant, the genie, the old blind men, and the animals that all waited inside her tale.

Scheherazade could not be cajoled or commanded to say another word. The teller of tales became as silent as the sword that hung between night and day, between life and death, between knowledge and blind sacrifice. For a moment that seemed longer than most, everything hung in the balance as the troubled king considered which way life would go and which way death.

Of course, the intrigue of the story prevailed and the sultan's power over life and death was suspended in favor of learning more about both. The desire for knowledge outweighed the blind pattern of vengeance. Caught in the enlivening narration, the young ruler was relieved of his compulsion to destroy life. The king agreed to wait until nightfall to hear the outcome of the tales of betrayal. The arc of anger and revenge was stilled, the new day arrived unencumbered by unnecessary sacrifice.

This world, they used to say, is made of nights and days. The way to sustain the world when all seems doomed is to fashion a bridge in the tension between opposing conditions, between night and day, between right and wrong, between love and hate. Scheherazade made a bridge of stories that held the end and beginning together. The king relinquished his desperate habits and was carried deeper and deeper into his own inner reflections.

The following night the storyteller picked up the thread of her tale and wove a tapestry of wonder, a veritable flying carpet made of endless intrigues. Meanwhile, the lives of Scheherazade and her sister were ransomed by the tales of the old blind men who were themselves redeeming the merchant with stories of their own heartaches. Each night she would spin more tales only to stop the flow of stories just before dawn. Each morning she would purchase another day for the daughters of the land and the peace of the country.

Each additional tale delayed death and saved a portion of life. Soon, the days began to follow the nights again in easy succession and the world seemed less desperate and meaningful life more possible. The stories continued for a thousand and one nights as the dense and wondrous fabric of tales slowly lifted the blindness from the eyes of the king and allowed the beauty and wonder of life to dawn again in his heart.

The tale told on the first night turned the literal situation of the king and the kingdom into a literary condition; it shifted the "facts of the matter" to a mythical context and broke open the blindness that had fallen over the whole land. In telling the tales of the blind men Scheherazade established that a story can be worth a life or at least a portion of it; that each life involves the living out and unraveling of a unique fate already present in the soul.

The wound at the center of the realm became approachable as the king's actual story was poured from one mythic container to another. Through the alchemy of storytelling the wounded ruler began to loosen the grip of vengeance and reach for the salve of understanding. Meanwhile, the teller's tales offered a mirror image of her own situation as her life also redeemed portions of story and ransomed insights into the maze of the human soul.

Suspending the sultan in the middle of a story helped move him back into the midst of life again. Scheherazade caught the grief-stricken and fallen king in the subtle nets of story. She pulled him with the thread of wonder onto a ground of possibility and began to turn him from the spell of death back to the song of life. The ruler had lost his soul and all reverence for life, but found it again in the medicine of the stories.

In knowing the way of stories, Scheherazade could intuit something of the sickness eating away at the heart of the king. She knew something of the remedy as well. For the cure lies close to the wound and a genuine medicine often partakes of the original poison. There was nothing else for it; she would have to drink from the same bitterness as the sick king in order to bring the remedy to bear.

Once a person begins to see with the poetic eye and feel with the sense of stories, the world reveals itself to be an endless tapestry woven of woe and wonder. Scheherazade saw in that way. She had the blessing of stories. Like it or not, she could hear the notes of fate and destiny in the music of danger. She had become a vessel of tales dealing with the torments and joys that crisscross the threshold of the human heart. She knew what the old people knew, that bitterness and wisdom cannot dwell in the same place. She knew that the bitterness in the heart of the king would have to be slowly drained if the sweetness of life was to return to the realm.

Although relatively young, he was fast growing old with bitterness and adding daily to his pain by inflicting suffering on others. A betrayal of the soul follows a person as dutifully as the animals in the story followed the blind men. As long as people remain blind to the conditions of their own souls they unconsciously practice a complicity in their own betrayal. Every betrayal has a portion of self betrayal in it. The king had been betrayed, but could not acknowledge his own guilt in the matter. The greatest betrayal occurs through the inner repetition of the guilt and pain of the original wound.

Scheherazade wove the wounded ruler back into the stories of the world. She pulled at his heart strings and loosened the bitterness that generated so much agony and death. She threaded the story of his loss and betrayal into tales that opened wide the territories of the human heart. She caught him in the World Behind the World and suspended the sword that kept cutting away at life. Her stories become the school in which the ruler's heart learned to love life again.

Scheherazade knew what the old tellers knew, that until we have a sense of the story trying to live through us we miss the meaning hiding in the wounds we carry. Without a storied sense of life we blindly continue to betray our own hearts and will wound others in predictable ways. Like the wounded, wounding king all must find threads of their own inherent tale in order to play a proper role on the stage of life.

Each heart walks innocently towards the swords of fate; each falls prey to inevitable betrayals and each betrays itself over and over like the love-damaged king until the inner story becomes better known. We are each the wounded and wounding king recklessly ruling the broken heart of our own lives. Each dawn we face the sword of awakening and the possibility of a reprieve that allows the soul to find its native voice and learn to sing again.

We are each the Vizier holding the sword that severs one thing from another, habitually creating false separations and bloody oppositions in our own lives and in the lives of our children. Each receives some blow from life and must struggle to heal the inner darkness that results from it. For life must be continually ransomed from the edge of darkness. People lose their heads over and over until awakening more fully to what really rules the heart and can ransom the soul from its inner exile.

We are each Scheherazade, knowing in some way that the realm has gone wrong and that something essential needs care and healing. For the world is ever our endangered sister. Until we pour our own story into the school of stories and mix it with tales that endure and help reveal meanings, we live a blindness that turn day into night and love into death. If those who hold the swords of power are not themselves held by the stories of life ongoing, then the balance of the whole world can tip towards death.

Salvation doesn't wait until the end of time; the divine doesn't suddenly appear after some final judgment. As Scheherazade demonstrates, it was there all along, hidden inside the pain, trapped by the tale of betrayal being told again and again within ourselves.

The pain of loss and betrayal at the beginning of the thousand and one nights serves as the symbolic wound of the entire realm and of all other earthly realms as well. All the rulers and all the daughters and sons of the world suffer with the same afflictions and ultimately seek similar medicines. When the internal ailments and divisions are not faced they enter the outer world and can become the fate of many. Whatever wounds the world has already been wounded.

When people or nations or cultures fall out of the stories that preserve the greater sense of life they become merchants of death by simple default. Death is the default position whenever the gift of life and the mysteries of love become overshadowed. In the end all stories are love stories; each life and each tale the residue of loving and not loving, each the result of striking blindly at life and trying to find the light of love in this world.

Some wounds cut so deeply that they sever the mind from the heart and cleave the soul in two. Some traumas leave people so split within that they can only see the world as utterly divided. Before it came to mean a holy war waged by true believers upon unbelievers, *jihad* referred to the battle being fought inside the human heart and soul.

Those caught in the blindness of fundamentalism hold their swords with the hands of their own wounds. In seeking to rid the world of the infidels and unbelievers, they cut themselves off from their own inner faithfulness. In desiring one form of faith to rule above all others they lose all real faith in the human heart. In seeking to find some guarantee of self-salvation they loose the hidden fidelity that secretly connects one heart to another.

The weapons of warring states and feuding religions are often sharpened on the inner despair of those who hold positions of power. Think of the wounded king again. In denying and avoiding his own pain he generated death and despair in the realm. There is a betrayal of the heart and of the spirit that occurs long before people take up the sword and pretend to separate others into believers and infidels. The sword of life and death hangs in the heart of humanity long before the shaping of theological and political arguments and mounting them up to take to battle. People slay each other in the mind and in the heart long before the bloody battles start.

Like any common person the king became most deeply divided where he would learn to love and be loved. Unable to surrender to his own pain, unwilling to seek for healing, he took up the sword and cut the world in two, so that the night knew nothing of the day and the day remained blind to the longings of the night.

The sword of denial swings back and forth between love and betrayal. Whatever and whomever he loved had to die before daylight might reveal the wound he could hide but not conceal. The desire for love he experienced each night had to be sacrificed before the light of day; for he cannot hold the two worlds together in his own heart, much less rule the realm with wisdom or compassion.

Having lost his faith in love, he placed his faith in destruction. The longing for a transcendent experience became a desire for death. He became a Disciple of the End and any who came too close found themselves in the "end-times."

The king fixated upon the inner experience of betrayal and only attended to that story. He only saw it one way and always saw it the same way. He becomes a fundamentalist fixated upon his own pain and obsessed with one way of seeing everything. Literalists and fundamentalists and true believers suffer in similar ways. Their blindness also reflects a one-eyed view of the world. They close the eye of insight and the door of self-reflection. They take one idea or a single story and see it literally as the true and only way to view this diverse and surprising world.

Each day they must sacrifice the possibilities of life in order to maintain an exacting but narrow and distorted way of being in the world. They misunderstand the saying that "narrow is the way," thinking that it suggests finding a straight and rigid approach to things divine. They forget the wider knowledge that reminds how all things, even pain, can connect a person to the divine.

Any path followed far enough can reach the divine, for divinity hides throughout the world and in unlikely places. The narrowness referred to in the old sayings had to do with the closeness between this world and the other. Think of the betrayed and betraying king. Each time he loved he had to kill what he loved; he had to destroy the evidence *that* he loved. His love and his hate were in the same place. Narrow is the way when a person must face the proximity of love and hate dwelling in his own breast. Each must risk the edge of his own hate to find the thread of his own love. In order to be healed the wound must pass through that narrow, cutting place in a new way.

Scheherazade opened the narrowness of the king with endless stories of love and hate, of faithfulness and deceit. She offered the mirror-sharp edge of the bridge of stories that can lead to the limitless territories that also inhabit the human heart. She did not tell the tales that end with "They lived happily ever after." Such fairy tales might suffice before the heart is truly broken; but for those fractured by love and torn by betrayal other tales are needed. The goal is not to find some heavenly ending like that promised to blind fanatics and desperate martyrs. The goal of life is to open the heart to eternity before death arrives.

Scheherazade knew enough to know that stories can help heal and make whole what cannot be held in any other way. She knew that she must hold together night and day and shape subtle bridges to the heart within the heart. In the course of a thousand and one nights, the wounded ruler entered the wild narratives of human love and human loss. He entered the stories as they entered him.

His heart breathed the curative air of the Otherworld. He wandered the fields of wonder, became abandoned on desert shores and lost in landscapes of exile and guilt until he found himself again in gardens of forgiveness. Over time the pattern of harshly splitting night and day dissolved, the hard heart softened again and learned to see how the two worlds are secretly connected and how wandering in one is also wandering in the other.

The goal of love is in the longing itself as day longs for night and darkness longs for dawn. In holding together the days and nights Scheherazade put the broken pieces of nobility back together again. As the young king came together in himself he and Scheherazade also joined together. From their complex intercourse over the thousand nights and one many things are born. The end of the thousand nights and one reveals that two children were born. From postponing one death, two births result. In the school of stories love blossomed between the storyteller and the ruler, between art and power. Scheherazade became mother as well as queen and savior of the kingdom.

Scheherazade brought the whole wound present with its capacity to keep wounding. She invited the full tension of the situation. She sharpened the sword and opened the wounds already present. She depended not on some technology or any specific theology. She trusted the world itself and the wisdom buried near the wounds of life. She opened the gates of suffering and invited the subtle presence of the Otherworld to shift the relationship between life and death.

Finding the right story can preserve life. In the end, even Death enjoys a good tale. Each life is worth more and becomes more worthy when understood as a story. Helping to save the world means finding wholeness again and finding wholeness requires suffering what has been divided within as well as what becomes conflicted in the outer world. Saving the realm means holding the darkness and the light together, not rejecting one and claiming the other.

To be fully alive each person must taste the bitterness of life and drink of the dregs of betrayal and loss. That's a rule on this earth where joy and despair appear on every threshold and secretly attend the opening of each door. Each of us carries a wounded ruler in our soul and each soul must drink from the cup of bitterness; yet each, surprisingly, carries a remedy within as well. Scheherazade counted upon that old medicine.

Against the literalism and blindness of the wounded king Scheherazade offered a thousand versions of the endless drama of the human heart. No single tale can neatly explain or resolve how the heart hardens and begins to attack the core of its own life. Each heart attack is different, just as each love affair must be. Yet every heart dwells within stories that reflect the eternal drama.

In the presence of genuine openness and wisdom even the most grievous offenses can find forgiveness. Like many others before and since, the wounded ruler had to forgive himself in order to see the harm he was creating. Through the tonic of stories he gained some understanding of his own heart. A renewed sense of forgiveness and justice and love soon followed in the wake of that healing.

There is no cure for love, except a person become a lover. No remedy for bitterness, except that wisdom dawn within. Either a person becomes wise and converts life's bitterness to medicine, or else becomes stuck in the dregs of betrayal and the haunts of self-pity. There is no cure for hate and bitterness except becoming wise, especially wiser about the story trying to live into the world through the longings of one's own soul.

CHAPTER 7

IN EXTREMIS

Beginnings and endings are the extremes of any story, the alpha and omega of any text. Typically, the beginning overflows with fresh potentials and unrealized possibilities that fill the immediate atmosphere with promise. Endings present the opposite extreme where life falters, things become undone, and the center can no longer hold. Not only does every issue tend to polarize everyone, but everything is taken to an extreme.

When it seems that the end is near extreme conditions become commonplace; not only extreme changes in the weather, but extremists of all kinds abound and exaggerated feelings develop inside people as well. And it's not just the religious extremists and the politics of extremism, but there are extreme makeovers, even extreme sports. The ends of time throw everyone and everything "in extremis."

Irrational influences and undue pressures become common and people feel driven to extremities, like it or not. It becomes difficult to avoid intense feelings and edgy thoughts as inner fears compete with outer threats. The end-times are when all is said and all is done, when all kinds of extreme possibilities appear and everything wants to be said and done at the same time.

When the forms of the world rattle, people have a tendency to grab something that seems solid or right and hold tightly to it. A single idea, a fixed principle, a unifying theory or a blind belief becomes preferable to the growing tension of opposing forces and conflicting opinions. Faced with radical changes and increasing uncertainties, many people hide behind a particular faith or a fixed ideology. The tendency to reduce the complexities of life and insist upon an absolute way of seeing things becomes stronger.

As things are taken to the extreme people run out of room, become inflexible, dig in, and hold on tight. Any issue considered must quickly become divided into opposing attitudes with one side claiming to be completely right and the other having to be utterly wrong.

At the absolute extremes no second thoughts are allowed, no second opinions needed, no more second chances either. Everything becomes carved in stone. Whoever doesn't see it that way is simply and irretrievably wrong and probably bad. Literalism, whether it be in science, politics, or religion, leads to blind alleys and dead ends, to final judgments and even "final solutions."

The true disease of the age is the rise of literalism and the corresponding loss of genuine imagination. For literalism reduces the world to fixed ideas and rigid dogmas while isolating people at the extremes of thought and belief. Literalism becomes a sword that divides things crudely, sometimes cruelly and creates false oppositions. Literalism is a form of forgetting; not simply a narrowing of vision, but a loss of insight, a trading of genuine reflection for simple facts or blind belief.

The habit of literalizing strikes religious fanatics and scientific realists alike. It spawns social ideologies, religious dogmas, and formulas of all kinds. Politicians, clergymen, and academics become enthralled with a single theory, a fixed idea, or a literalized story. Soon the teeming world of creation has been reduced to a single-minded, one-eyed view. Whole populations come to simply "believe" one way or another. As if believing made something true, as if belief meant more than genuine knowledge, as if wisdom didn't require being able to hold more than one view at the same time.

Literalism has two factions that often oppose each other vehemently while secretly conspiring to reduce the mystery of the living world. One side champions positivism and a tyranny of scientism that obsesses over facts and figures and relies solely upon a statistical world view. The opposite extreme insists upon fundamental religious beliefs that reject facts or alter them to conform with literalized stories. Some stick to the facts as held by the hard sciences, while others insist upon fixed beliefs enshrined in exacting dogmas.

One side becomes nihilistic and can't really believe in anything at all, while the other side believes one thing no matter what evidence to the contrary might say, believes all the more because what it believes cannot be verified. Each side tries to prove the foolishness of the other, yet each remains literalist in its own way. These are two sides of the same concretized coin. Each views the world with a single vision and can't quite open the eye of imagination or loosen the mind enough to become "double-minded."

Each side gains some surety at the cost of a tragic loss of imagination and a dramatic reduction in the sense of wonder at the immediate world. Literalism takes the mystery out of life and eventually takes the life out of the mysteries. From there, it's a short journey to expecting the whole thing to end at any moment. Literalist attitudes in modern sciences and within mass religions lead people to envision an actual end to the created world, albeit for different reasons.

When simple belief replaces wonder and fear replaces the awe proper to seeing the beauty and surprise of life, then something essential has been lost. The loss of wonder for the living world and awe at being part of it grows as part of the cost of literal thinking, be it scientific positivism or religious fundamentalism. As wonder becomes reduced to the facts of the matter or restricted to fixed beliefs, the end of the world seems near indeed, either a fact to be reckoned with or a necessary evil to await.

Those who lose the mythic sense become fascinated with things that only make sense in limited ways. In referring to the facts of the matter they miss the sense of the story. In denying the complexity of the world they miss the divine aspects already present within it. Meanwhile, the hardest facts turn out to be partly fictional and the absolute beliefs can't purchase a portion of heaven.

Those who take the world to be simply literal or only a fallen place miss the fractal renewals playing at the edges of reality. For in this world of stories even the hard facts can turn out to be fiction, while the most outrageous fictions can come closest to the truth. This world is both a matter of fact and the stuff of fiction. What people call the world is both created and made up, it evolves from nothing and can continually be recreated from moment to moment, from epoch to epoch, from story to story, from breath to breath.

The Unknown has always been the companion of the living. And seen mythically, this world continues to be a locus of mystery and life remains an act of wonder in which some risk attends each breath and the necessity of love trumps all theories. The facts are never enough to explain the mysteries of the heart or the wonders of the mind; never enough to grasp the living edge that stretches between the two worlds.

It isn't that facts and measurements don't matter, rather that they can never tell the whole story. At one level, knowing the facts of life becomes necessary for survival. Sometimes the facts matter more than anything else; and sometimes the facts don't matter much at all. Settling for the world of appearances reduces life to obvious proportions and can precipitate more tragedy than is necessary.

It used to be better known that common reality offers a world of appearances; that behind all appearances stands the Real behind the real. In mistaking appearances for the Real, people wind up with the appearance of strength, the appearance of power, the appearance of leadership, the appearance of freedom, the appearance of meaning while suffering a loss of all that is truly meaningful in the end.

THE GIFT OF LIFE

The ancient Mayan creation story, the Popul Vuh or Council Book, offers a glimpse of how the hardheaded style of literalism might have entered this world. And it offers a vision of how people might find again the great imagination that centers people between the solid ground of the earth and the unseen realm that sustains it.

The ancient Mayans considered creation to be an ongoing project; that the original sound and word of creation continues to ripple forth from the beginning; that the song of making continues to murmur and sigh throughout the world even now. For them, the eloquence of creation speaks its living language throughout the daily world and whispers wisely inside the old stories.

The eloquence of life was hidden behind appearances at the very beginning when only the sky was open and the face of the earth was not yet clear. At that time there was only the heavenly world above and its reflection upon the sea that looked up to it. At that time nothing stirred, everything was waiting, still held back behind a veil of silence.

The world was a hidden unity waiting to speak and the first words would change everything by bringing the hidden to the fore. It was then that the original thinkers joined their words and their thoughts. They had names like Heart of Heaven, Heart of Sky, Heart of Earth, Hurricane, and Sudden Thunderbolt. Some say that there was only one being speaking at the beginning, others say that the One spoke with many voices. One or many, take your choice, everyone agrees that the speaking had to begin and that the naming still continues in the darkness behind things and in the voice of every dawn.

The original thinkers thought and worried over creation. They conceived the growth of mountains, the generation of trees, the pulsing of animals, the eruption of all life forms at the beginning when everything was possible. They say that after being at creation for a while, Heart of Heaven desired that the gift of life be recognized on earth; that gratitude become part of the expressed eloquence of existence.

Yet somehow the animals were unable to pronounce all that the creators desired to hear. Their sounds and even their songs couldn't express a certain knowledge that was needed to complete the song of creation. Something was missing in the great garden of the incarnated world causing Heart of Heaven to ponder and consider that absence.

With the idea of more expressive creatures in mind, Heart of Heaven shaped some beings from mud, from some clay that was already there. These "mud beings" were interesting: they had unique shapes and soft contours. That turned out to be a problem with them, they were simply too soft. When the rains came those mud people became mushy and soon melted right back into the earth.

Heart of Heaven allowed the rain to melt them down and soon fashioned some new creatures from wood and from hollow reeds. The new creatures were an improvement; they were able to walk about and soon began making things themselves. In some ways they reflected the ongoing creation. They spent their time making things, even developing primitive ideas and related technologies. The "wood people" were superior to the mud people, they didn't melt when it rained and they stood up for themselves.

However, it turned out that the wood people lacked hearts and their minds were as narrow as reeds. They turned out to be hardheaded and couldn't manage to be openhearted. They were like "doll people." Yes, they could make things, but they did not remember their own maker and could not provide the expression of gratitude and appreciation for life that had been the inspiration for their creation. Even the animals sensed that something was wrong with the doll people and eventually rebelled against them and their technologies.

It was as if everything in creation spoke out against them; the animals and the trees and even their own utensils eventually turned upon them. Soon, Heart of Heaven caused a thick rain of black water to fall and the doll people were scattered and destroyed. Some say that the survivors of those made from wood became monkeys and continue to live in this world.

Heart of Heaven wasn't finished with the notion of creating creatures conscious of the gift of life. It seems that even at the beginning, things had to be attempted three times before the hidden could become visible. Heart of Heaven decided to fashion some creatures using corn or maize as the basic material. Heart of Heaven shaped some maize into dough, breathed some life into it and soon the "corn people" were born.

Right from the beginning the people made of maize were different. The primary distinction involved their ability to see. The corn people were the first creatures to look past their immediate condition and see beyond the immediate needs. They survived all the storms of life and became the ancestors of all the people who came to life after that time. They survived and thrived on earth because of their awareness of the world. For they had enough insight to immediately recognize the gift of life and the wonders of creation.

The corn people felt gratitude in their hearts and approached the world with respect. They found artful ways to express appreciation for the gift of life. Heart of Heaven became pleased with this turn of events and it seemed that the missing piece of creation had been added. However, another problem soon developed. Some people say that there is always one problem after another. Some even believe that the problems in the world keep creation going along.

At any rate, the new beings, our common ancestors, had a remarkable ability to see into the very heart of the world. They could see beyond the forests in which they dwelt. They had great vision; they were both farsighted and had second sight. They could see beyond the obvious and see deep within themselves. Their sight made them knowledgeable of the earth and of the ways of creation. Not only could they recognize the creators, but they could see in ways that were similar to the vision characteristic of the early deities.

That capacity for great vision was a primary power and ability for the first real ancestors of humanity; but it also became the source of some discomfort for the gods of creation. For it soon seemed that the corn people would become the equal of the gods. That troubling possibility caused the early deities to ask Heart of Heaven to reduce the vision of the people. They asked that the people have more short-term vision and less ability to see the way the creators saw things.

Heart of Heaven agreed and the vision of the ancestors was reduced to the ways that people tend to see even now. However, Heart of Heaven added one stipulation. The people would have their vision diminished, but they would have access to the stories of creation and to the images that appeared when everything was just beginning to appear. Humans would have a "seeing instrument," a kind of book that would allow them to see with genuine vision. By attending to the original thoughts with open hearts and minds, the living people could open the eyes of true vision again and see in ways that helped creation to continue.

Because of that stipulation everyone continues to be born with the capacity to imagine and see beyond the immediate needs and past the limits of self-involvement. As descendents of the corn people humans remain capable of far-sight, of in-sight, and second-sight, yet tend to awaken in that way only after other approaches have failed them. Often it takes three tries before something becomes revealed to human sight or to human thought. Often people must enter the great stories again in order to see the world in its divine proportions.

Like the vestigial tail that reminds people that they are connected to animals at one end, the capacity for great imagination connects people to the gods at the other extreme. When living people can hold those extremes together they become the friends of creation, the companions of the animals, and a living expression of gratitude for the gift of life.

Genuine people only appeared after two failed attempts as if to indicate that people might fail in life before finding the right way to go. Even then, being successful can disrupt the balance of creation. The beginning sets the pattern for all that follows; to this day, many artists destroy what they make with their own hands before finding the proper shape and meaning of their work. For better or worse we invent faulty utensils and indulge in patterns that threaten the very elements of creation. For better or worse we sometimes see as the gods see, for what was given cannot simply be taken away.

There are the times when the dark rain comes again and humanity seems to regress and walk backwards through the phases of creation. In the great recycling of time phases of the old story come around again and the blindness of humanity troubles the earth, threatens the divine, and offends the animals as well.

Under the guise of progress clever utensils and technological advancements can mimic the mistakes of the doll people in being short-sighted as well as hard-hearted. The notion that technology alone might save the world misses the point that short-sighted inventions and technological solutions often isolate people from nature while narrowing the options for genuine survival. Unless the capacity for technical invention be placed in service of the long vision and the ongoing story of creation it still tends to turn the natural world against us.

When times become troubled and the hard rain falls people tend to regress. Some become softheaded and halfhearted; they are too easily dismayed and can't stand up to the forces of change. Faced with great challenges they become overly adaptive and too easily manipulated. At the first sign of trouble they are to ready to melt into the background, relinquish their uniqueness, and become part of the crowd, neither responsible for anything, nor responsive to life.

Others go to the opposite extreme and become rigid in their attitudes and lack insight like the doll people who had no real hearts or minds. They attack what they don't understand, make war on nature, even on diseases and try to master fear with tools of terror. Literalism, fundamentalism, materialism and all the other "isms" partake in the hardheaded narrowness that characterized the doll people and caused nature and the animals to turn against them.

It's an old story told many times, how people present a strange mixture of godlike vision and mudlike limitations. How humans are made from the infinite heart of heaven, yet how individuals must struggle mightily to open their own hearts and minds. We stand upright by virtue of root connections to the heart of the earth, yet often can't see the forest for the trees. Like the original creators, humans experiment with elements of this world and make puzzling mistakes as dazzling inventions and seemingly important ideas turn to mud in our hands.

Some modern people consider humans an afterthought of creation and unnecessary for life on earth to continue. The old stories see it differently. Humans are a risk taken by the forces of creation in the interest of conscious awareness and genuine vision on earth. In order to make beings that could understand the value of life the gods had to generate them from the very heart of creation and then run the risk that they would trouble the world with their visionary powers and delusional states.

By virtue of the original dispensation, all persons have a speck of "god-sight" as well as specific ways of being blind to the world and their place within it. Humans remain connected to the heart of heaven and to the heart of earth even when they don't fully know it. The eloquence of the beginning resides in the human soul but only awakens in critical times and in creative moments. There's some sense in the idea that a flood of changes might force a return to the origins and to a renewed reverence for the gift of life.

There's some encouragement in the notion that the gods of creation made mistakes at the beginning. There's some hope in the idea that people could awaken from the wooden-headed conditions that generate harsh technologies, that threaten the animals and offend the deities. There's a troubled possibility that after recognizing how hard-headed and hard-hearted culture has become people might find some insights into the heart of the earth and cease to offend the rest of creation.

THE ORIGINAL MISTAKE

Some religions have trouble with the notion that the creator makes mistakes and has to learn the ropes of creating. Everything has to start somewhere and the idea of mistakes made during creation offers an alternative to the punishment predicted with an "original sin." If creation includes mistakes from the very beginning, then the myriad of mistakes continuing to be made in this world make more sense. If the problems of the world stem from an original mistake, then all of our mistaken ideas and mindless pursuits become more understandable and more forgivable.

Accepting that rather big errors were part of the world from the beginning allows creation to continue despite all the damning errors and ongoing tragedies. Consider the Garden of Eden with the notion that mistakes have to be made and have to begin when things are just beginning. The original people have to do everything for the first time. Eve and Adam make the first big mistake and the most common human mistake; for they desire to know what the gods know. Right or wrong, that desire was there at the beginning, just as it exists now.

The paradoxical first pair were shaped in such a way that they were bound to try to see the way the gods see and bound to make mistakes while learning to have genuine gratitude for the gift of life. Like everyone who has followed them down the forbidden roads of knowledge, their sin turns out to be their gift, a gift from god and an offense to the gods as well.

To this day, if you want people to desire something strongly, just call it forbidden fruit. Anyone could have known that the way to guarantee that people become intrigued with something is to forbid them to go near it. That's basic human psychology, part of the setup, built into people from the very beginning. Any creating deity should know that part. Humans have an inborn desire to see and know as the gods do.

Pointing to a certain tree where the fruits of knowledge hang within easy reach provokes a desire that was already there. Forbidding the tasting of that fruit turns out to be the most certain way to initiate the harvesting of it. Eve and Adam made a necessary mistake. They triggered the search for knowledge and that turns out to be the only way to learn genuine gratitude for the gift of life.

It's one thing to have an abundance of earthly creatures, quite another to fashion creatures with curiosity, with natural ambition and a capacity to see into eternity. Attempting that upsets the original garden and threatens to undermine everything; yet unless such things occur there can be no real gratitude for life and no genuine forgiveness either. In order to share in the knowledge of creation and awaken to genuine gratitude the new creatures must wander close to divine vision. Call them the maize people, call them the first couple, the First People, the Ancients, the ancestors, like god they have many names.

Remember old Prometheus? He stole the fire of the gods and gave it to humans. Prometheus means "farsighted," "able to see ahead." Whether it be the fruit of knowledge, the fire of heaven or the gift of divine sight, most old stories depict the ancestors as burning with longings and burdened with visions. Humans enter the song of creation both gifted and wounded, both inspired and mistaken, the paradoxical inheritors of paradise found and paradise lost.

When the chaos of the end beckons and the underlying issues of creation rise closer to the surface, humans repeat the original patterns that include serious mistakes as well as possibilities of penetrating visions. In a strange way, humans are the friends as well as the enemies of creation and, at some level also the envy of the gods. Jealous gods can turn against their own creatures making the search for genuine vision and meaning more treacherous and complicated.

The gods may resent the vision of mankind, yet creation seems to require such visionaries. Call it a sin, call it an unavoidable mistake, either way humans are implicated in the problems and in the solutions when dissolution seems at hand.

Those who see things in narrow and fundamentalist ways become stuck like the doll people when the winds of change blow strongly. Scientific positivists and true believers of all kinds become stuck at the level of creation where they see things only one way. Unable to see the way nature constantly shifts and changes and recycles, they cling to a single-eyed vision of the world and wind up at odds with the rest of creation. When another stage of life comes along they see it as The End, because the way they see must end as another vision of the world ensues.

THE EYE OF THE HEART

True vision requires an open heart as well as an open mind. The human heart is the organ at issue in the current dilemmas, just as it was in the beginning. The heart is a subtle organ that remains connected to the Heart of Heaven and to the Heart of the Earth.

People are made to see beyond the obvious; shaped to see double in order to have depth of vision. Yet there are greater depths than that; there are inner eyes that see everything differently. Our vision, like our speech, is meant to be metaphorical, able to see and communicate things beyond any measure. The eye of the heart is shaped for seeing the mysteries of life and love and for sighting new ways for making both.

The inner eyes see everything metaphorically. We call a certain person lion-hearted, another is eagle-eyed, a third has the stomach of an ox. In the strange weaving together of human organs with animal intensities people capture things that are there, yet can't be proven. Humans are half animal and half other. The other part can be godlike or else act worse than any animal. Humans are required to bear the presence of inhuman things and experience the extremes of being.

Some might argue that the heart and the eye are separate organs that shouldn't be confused. One receives impressions of light and movement; the other, deeply encased in the body, is there to pump blood. Yet, there are organs within organs. The mind can be anywhere in the body; a blind person can see many things clearly. The heart can see and has its own sense of purpose and direction. It has its own thoughts that began long before the mud body formed and all the kicking and crying started.

That heart's eye was open before birth. It saw otherworldly things and seeks to perceive them again. The pain of birth closed that eye, yet it expects to open again in the course of life. Trying to see that way again requires that the heart crack wider open and that brings back the original pain of separation from the divine. Many try to avoid that heart-breaking pain; yet, the eye of the heart can only see through cracks in this world.

It used to be better known that the only heart worth having is a broken heart. Only then can others find a way in, only then do people develop insight into their own wound and its healing. The heart becomes embattled within long before the heart attack ensues. A doctor who doesn't know the subtleties of the organ within the organ is simply a surgeon of the obvious; he may be doing emergency work, but the pathways of real healing remain obstructed.

The heart is first of all a metaphorical organ. It has foresight as well as hindsight. It has insight and remains subject to visions right up to the end. The heart is a measureless territory trying to open to greater and greater awareness. Refusing to see with the inner eyes makes a person blind to the way that life and death pass back and forth in each moment. Each moment we die and come back to life, in the blink of an eye, in the exchanges of blood in the inner chambers of the heart.

The heart knows this passage back and forth and the knowledge found between. Seen with that eye, death becomes the way we grow, continually dying to one way of seeing in order to find a greater vision. The eye of the heart is made to see beyond, to glimpse the whole cosmos and perceive its own paradoxical place in that great arrangement. The human heart is a great inner territory that participates in creation, and that makes mistakes, yet can learn to forgive itself and forgive others as well.

If the heart doesn't open to its own vision and learn the meaning already hidden within, it can become a weapon that battles with all of creation. Many things can close and harden the heart. Extremes of poverty can dry the heart and turn it bitter. Too much rejection can cause persons to reject their own inner vision. Violation of the subtle tissues of the heart can turn it towards violence, and too much sorrow makes a stone of the heart.

When the space between common reality and the greater heart vision becomes too wide, people can't perceive the subtle presence of the unseen in this earthly world. There follows a loss of imagination, a blindness that leaves people trying to measure everything to determine what might be real.

In a sense, the first people were also the last experiment of creation. In many old tales humans were the last creatures made and therefore the youngest children of the earth. Seen that way humans are the culmination of the creative effort, both the end of the line and the height of creation. This image repeats in many fairy stories and folk tales where the youngest sister or youngest brother seems out of touch and least able to be helpful in the conventional world.

The youngest doesn't measure up, being too much caught in dreams or too weird in their ways. They seem aimed another way and don't see the world in normal terms; they don't fit the mold and fail to follow the conventional paths. Yet when it all seems about to end and end badly, the visionary capacities and surprising resources of the youngest become necessary for everyone's survival.

When everything seems most threatened and all the usual methods and practical patterns lead to disaster and dead ends, when most people melt into the masses while others harden their attitudes, the youngest sister and brother hidden in the heart wake up. When the world seems weary with ignorance and threatened by the hardening of minds and hearts, the eternal youth in the heart tries to awaken to visions that connect all the way back to the beginnings of time.

In the end, the human soul tries to become ancient again and being ancient means having the courage of beginnings as well as the wisdom of survival. Not the simple survival of the fittest, but an awakening of surprising visions that don't fit within literal ways of seeing. The eloquence of creation and meaningful imagination waits to be found where it always resides in the heart within the heart, in the living stories that reconnect the mind and the heart.

III

The Song of the Chaosmos

CHAPTER 8

FOLK MYTHS AND OPEN SECRETS

This world teems with tales of creation, and floods with stories about how things end. Most cultures have more than one origin story; even the Bible offers two ways of seeing the beginning. So many ways to view creation and endless narrations of its demise! Yet no exact beginning means no final end. That's the mythic perspective and this world is a mythic place before it becomes anything else.

Great civilizations begin with mythic narrations and symbols that help to establish them and shape their unique message. Over time the origin stories can become a matter of literal belief, even become recast as historical fact. The original imagination runs dry as once powerful states slip back towards the roots of history. Great monuments and temples eventually backslide into the folds of the earth's garment. The once-amazing oases of civilization and the deep rivers of religious conviction begin to diminish, to dry out and return to the sands of time. Whatever claims a specific beginning in time will come to its end in due time.

Whereas the grand myths and epic sagas tend towards historical conclusions and often predict tragic endings, more humble folk myths tend to escape the final chapter and survive to another day. Survival is a keynote of folk tales and a habit of the common folk, just as it is a core practice of

Nature itself. Folk myths and genuine folklore offer artful ways to survive the repeated disasters and inevitable collapses of high culture.

Folk myths carry the same seeds of imagination and inspiration that give rise to the epic historicized tales; they just carry them more simply. Alongside the parade of major civilizations and the processions of the great religions, the tracks of the common folk can be found, a bit in the shadows and closer to the dust of the road. They carry the folk lore and local tales more closely connected to the land and to the knowledge of specific places. Attending more to earthly lore than codified law, they draw upon wisdom, traditions, and the old roots of earth knowledge.

Village tales and folk myths linger on the edges of civilization like intelligent animals waiting to be recalled or like crucial memories tucked away until a time of need arrives. They wait for the trouble to get deep and for people to wonder whether this has ever happened before. Like the animals, the folk of folk tales are long-term inhabitants of the earth and friendly reminders that what troubles us most deeply has happened before and that people have survived to tell the tale.

The folk of folklore tend to have little myths of how the world survives rather than grand dramas of how it all comes to an end. When the great civilizations lose their civility and collapse upon the historical heap, the folk continue along intuitively, instinctively making do with remnants, loose ends and leftovers that remain when everything falls apart. When the end seems near it might be wiser to turn to the lore of survival and the humble but enduring tapestries of stories that don't quit and tales that can't end.

Although indigenous to a particular area to begin with, the mythic motifs of folk tales can suddenly appear anywhere in the world. The essential characters of folk myths are both indigenous and indigent; they wander from place to place, yet remain connected to invisible roots that tie them to soul of the world. The folk of folktales are the original survivalists and they survive by remembering the age-old pattern of life, death, and renewal that ultimately sustains both great nature and human culture.

Folk tales can fall out of fashion where high cultures lose touch with the root stories and root metaphors of primordial imagination. Though simple and often rough in appearance, folk and fairy tales carry basic and essential knowledge of the world and how to survive in it. The animals, the "little folk," the wise old women, and sage old men in stories carry threads of knowing that constitute the wisdom of the earth. Folk tales are a part of the open secrets of life; part of an earthly wisdom that avoids the dizzying heights of culture by keeping close to the ground of being.

Though easily overlooked, often looked down upon, or relegated to the children's corner, folk myths live outside the narrow entrapments of civilized theologies and cultural ideologies and therefore survive the unraveling of those grand schemes. Like dreams and poetry, they are part of the "there-not-there" quality of this world. They are an aspect of culture, yet not too cultivated. They are connected to nature and have a strong sense of place, yet they deal with shape-shifting and radical transformations.

They inhabit an intermediate realm between high myth and common sense. They shelter an uncommon sensibility that involves both a sense of survival and an awareness of the little redemptions that keep things going along even when everything seems about to collapse altogether.

Unlike religious fables or scientific theories folk myths don't require that we believe in them; they prefer that we continue to learn from them. No one can own them or even fully interpret them. They are easily handled, readily translated, and suffer misuse rather casually. They don't resist being elaborated into morality tales or abducted into holy books. They survive being mishandled by distracted parents and illustrated by clumsy draftsmen. No matter, they survive and recall to us what is so readily forgotten in the centers of the great cultures, left out of the classic compilations of history and overlooked in the long-shadowed halls of academia.

Mythic symbols and primordial ideas live amongst the folk long after they have been argued out of the halls of the scholars. They continue to inspire long after the great libraries have been ransacked and the museums reduced to mausoleums. For knowledge cannot completely disappear; if it does become lost it returns to the realm of stories where it waits to be recalled and become useful again.

Folk myths comprise an inner text that lends itself to literary as well as religious writings. They harbor ideas and images that can be elaborated to operatic levels and become the grand symbols of ascending cultures. They form a "loose literature" that inhabits the soul of the world and that survives the ravaging of the temples of knowledge by unbelievers and believers alike. Being neither great literature nor divine word, they can return to the nomadic campfires and forest haunts when the great civilizations collapse, as they all eventually do.

Old stories persist like those mysterious paintings hidden deep in the caves of old Mother Earth. When the ideas and beliefs of a given time wear thin and fail to carry the collective longings of people, core stories continue to encourage, inspire, and instruct those willing to listen and hear them anew. Their wisdom is only available to those foolish enough to wander off the beaten paths and remain for a time in the bush or near the hearth of the ancient human village.

These days we are in folk-tale conditions again. Like characters in a story we cannot escape the trouble we have gotten into. The only way out is to go through it and the only way to go through it is to find some wisdom right here on earth, the way the enduring characters of folk myths continue to do.

FOOLISH WITH DREAMS

Remember old Noah who had to hold onto a dream and foolishly fashion a ship for a flood that had not yet appeared? He was a mythical character in folk traditions long before being drafted to play a role in anyone's religion. He set sail in many places before winding up in the biblical seas. He first began dreaming of floods and building arks in tales that were older than time itself. The idea of things beginning with a dream, the need to include all the animals and the whole notion of surviving the end are features of folk myths found throughout the world.

Flood stories have been found all over the earth, even in landlocked places; as if to say that it is not exactly the literal seas that are being addressed, but the psychic waters of the unconscious that can flood forth and overwhelm an individual or a culture at any time. Noah is one name for the old survivor in human awareness that keeps close to animals and the elements of nature. Old Noah is part of the inner nature of human nature, part of the original nature and surviving capacity of the human soul.

Rather than being an historical figure or a religious model, old Noah remains an inner resource, an indelible, unsinkable inhabitant of the human story and part of the imaginative inheritance of every living person. When people start to talk again about the loss of the world or the end of time, the old sailor stirs again inside the human psyche. Noah stands for the timeless dreamer in the human soul who knows what to do when the floods of change gather and the sense of dissolution grows.

Noah is the ancient mariner of the soul ever setting sail on swollen seas at the behest of one god or another. For Noah served many gods before reaching the desert sands and parchment pages of the Bible. "This has all happened before," says the old dreamer in the guise of Noah or Utnapishtim or Manu. Noah is only one of many names for the ancestral faculty for invention and instinct for survival that continue to inhabit the old soul hidden within humanity.

Some say that Utnapishtim was the first Noah; certainly he was a predecessor who faced an earlier flood. At that time they say that the earth was troubled by overpopulation and a shocking increase of ignorance. There were increasing numbers of people who increasingly failed to recognize the presence of the divine in the immediate world. Short-term thinking overruled greater imaginations and those who held the positions of authority had become blind to the wonders of the earth and the subtleties of the soul. Amidst a decrease of gratitude, a coarsening of culture and the growth of cynicism, things were going from bad to worse.

Enlil was the leader of the gods at that time. He was said to be born from a union of the sky and the earth and to have both a capacity to be distant and an inclination to get involved in what transpired on earth. The name *Enlil* means "lord wind" and true to his nature, the god decided to clean things up and wash everything pure again by sending torrential storms and thoroughly flooding the earth with water.

Amongst the people of that time, Utnapishtim was an exception. He retained a true sense of wonder about life and awe for the divine elements he saw on earth. And, Utnapishtim was a dreamer. People have always dreamed, sometimes little dreams that simply recast elements of the previous day, sometimes big dreams intended to change lives, even save lives. Utnapishtim was visited by big dreams and was wise enough to pay attention to them. One night he dreamed of a great deluge and a flood over the face of the earth.

The dream included the image of a sturdy ship and he lost no time building one. He gathered some helpers and together they managed to fashion a large vessel and load it with family and friends, as well as "the seed of all living creatures," even including the wild animals.

Soon heavy rains did come down and the waters rose up as it stormed for six wild days. In the fury of the deluge even the gods became frightened. Hordes of people and herds of animals drowned day after day and the massive loss of life caused the gods to repent and weep amongst themselves. By then, the waters covered the entire earth except for the very top of Mount Nisur which remained above the flooding tide. The storm carried the ship laden with dreams and people and animals right to that high peak where it could wait out the raging storm.

Utnapishtim means "he who found life" and it was he who had to find a way to bring life back to the earth when the flood finally began to subside. He decided to release a dove to see if it would find some dry land, but the dove soon returned to the ship having found nowhere else to settle. After a time he sent a sparrow out, but it too flew wearily back. Finally, Utnapishtim released a raven. When it did not return he knew that the waters had receded enough for the people and the animals to emerge from the vessel.

Many creation stories begin with an endless expanse of water and re-creation tales often depict everything returning to a fluid state before the next phase of life can begin. In some tales a white dove brings an olive branch to indicate that the waters have subsided and peace has returned to the earth. In others a dark raven returns with something scavenged from dry land.

The idea isn't to believe in a particular version of the flood story or any of the other core tales that sustain human imagination and inspire timely ingenuity. The point of creation tales and salvation stories is to awaken the dreamer in the soul and call upon the human capacities for awe and wonder and reverence for the involvement of the divine in the here and now.

A loss of gratitude for the gift of life and a growing ignorance of how the divine remains involved with the earth typically precipitate the great flood tales. Something similar happens when individuals have lost their connection to the unseen and resist initiatory changes trying to enter their lives. People dream of tidal waves, of having to swim in rough waters or else of drowning in dark seas. Often a genuine solution is preceded by a dissolution as consciousness dissolves back to the primal seas from which it first arose.

The percentage of water in the human body reflects the proportion of water found over the earth. The human psyche behaves like water; it flows, even floods with ideas, images, and dreams. It changes shape depending on the situation, can adjust to most terrains and occasionally becomes dammed up as well. Offering a drink of water used to be considered a natural courtesy and a way of offering peace. Water has always been sacred to humanity and reflective of the presence of the soul.

Flood stories are connected to the old practices of libation and baptism where intentional washing in water was used to cleanse the heart and remove disturbances from the mind. Before it became a circumscribed ceremony that happened only once in life, baptism was a ritual repeated whenever a person or a group became overly conflicted or deeply confused. Instinctively, people have immersed themselves in water as a way of reconciling their spirit and starting life over again. Those who believe in being born again from the waters of baptism repeat an old idea. The oldest version of that kind of renewal involved being born again, and again, and again.

The basic elements of life often shape core practices and provide essential symbols for unifying both the heart and the mind. The mountaintop that stood above the waters of dissolution and change offers the oldest image of an earthly temple and a primordial symbol of the earth itself as a temple rising above the troubles of the times. Being on top of a mountain meant being close to the heavenly realms where the deities dwell. In many old stories a single tree stands at the peak. Thus, the original steeple, the first minaret, the ancient stupa appears as the Tree of Life undamaged by even the floods of change.

The temple of the earth with its holy Tree of Life stands at the center of many old tales as if to indicate that when things become dark and treacherous on earth, it is time to find the center again. At the center, life can renew itself and new solutions can be found amidst the great dissolutions that turn everything upside down.

On the highest point of the earth Utnapishtim made a sacrifice to all the gods for allowing the people and the animals to be saved from extinction. In making the prayers of gratitude he included all the gods that were known and any that might be unknown. Some say that supplications to the known and unknown shape the oldest known prayers. Another old prayer form involved asking for forgiveness both for known mistakes and for any mistakes made, but not yet known.

Like myths and stories, prayers can take an endless number of shapes and forms. People used to fashion prayers from the ingredients of the moment and from whatever words happened to gather at the root of the tongue. Some say that a simple acknowledgement of something in the world greater than oneself constitutes a prayer. Each bow to the unseen and each expression of gratitude for the gift of life makes a prayer whether the seas be calm at the moment or stirred by storms.

Having made appropriate prayers, Utnapishtim and the company of survivors began to populate the earth again. After that the old dreamer and his wife received the gift of immortality and were given a place to live in peace at the "ends of the earth." It was the old dreamer and sailor Utnapishtim that the famous king Gilgamesh sought to find when his life dissolved in grief and loss. Gilgamesh sought to find a branch of the Tree of Immortality and had to go to the ends of the earth where Utnapishtim dwelt, where the ends of time touched the roots of the eternal and the old dreamer sleeps and wakes.

When the seas of change and times of loss sweep over the world again, the awakening of the inner dream of life becomes the issue. Like Noah and Utnapishtim, each soul begins the great journey of life with a dream. Each soul sails forth from the unseen on a dream that carries it across the threshold of life when the waters break at the onset of the birth labors. The inner dream is the vessel for the entire project of each foolish life. It's the only safe haven when the storms rage and the floods of change come around and even the gods must weep.

When the usual solutions fail to keep things afloat and the mainstream becomes flooded with anomalies, it becomes more important to follow a dream like old Noah. It becomes wiser to reconnect to the intuitive and instinctive realm the way animals sense a storm coming and head for higher ground. Noah is the part of each person that intuits when to depart from the mainstream and seek unfamiliar tributaries of knowledge.

As the floods of uncertainty rise in the world again, it helps to remember old Noah and Utnapishtim and all the old dreamers and survivors that are the true ancestors of humanity. They maintained the secret bond with Nature and the animals and they held the earth to be a temple and any meaningful change to be a baptism. In stories found all over the world they continue to suggest that something dreaming within us best knows how to shape a vessel for the troubles and tribulations of our exact lives.

Those who believe in literal versions of mythical stories and go looking for evidence of the old arks and the routes followed by supposedly historical characters miss the point intended by "it came in a dream," or "god whispered in his ear." The conversations that lead to the little redemptions that sustain life begin in some strange and unique way. To the common eye or the orthodox view Noah was anything but normal. In the end each person must learn the language through which the unseen world speaks to them.

MANU AND THE FISH OF GOD

The story of Manu and the Little Fish offers another old version of the flood story. In ancient Hindu myths Manu was the first human. His name suggests "man" and "mankind," but also has roots meaning "to think." Manu was the original thinker, the first thoughtful human ancestor. Manu represents an original pattern in the human soul, an archetypal prototype that remains part of the human imagination and mythic inheritance.

Once, near the very beginning of time, Manu had something on his mind and went to walk along the shore of a sea where the dense earth was washed by endless waves. Ever since, people often feel more free and open when walking the shores of oceans, lakes, and streams. Thoughts flow more easily there and the inner climate can shift and sift through possibilities at the subtle edge that is neither one thing nor the other.

Instinctively, Manu bent down to wash his hands in the old gesture of libation and submission. Suddenly, a small fish appeared and begged him for protection from the larger fish intent on swallowing it. This happened long ago, close to the origins of life, when it was easier for animals and humans to communicate.

Even at that early time the pattern of big fish eating little prevailed; it was part of things from the very beginning. Big fish eats little, large devours small in the teeming seas of life where one thing feeds upon another. The pattern continues to this day, found throughout nature as well as in every culture of the earth.

The fish told Manu that if he offered help on this occasion it would return the favor when he faced death and disaster. Manu reached down, collected the little fish in his hands and carried it home. It was a small thing to do, a simple gesture of sympathy; yet there was something significant in the connection between the two species and the way they carried on together.

Manu placed the fish in a jar and cared for it. A little nourishment and attention caused it to grow rapidly and soon it outgrew its jar. Manu had to transfer it to a bigger container, but it soon it grew too large for that. Manu had to find bigger and bigger reservoirs for the ever expanding fish. He carried it to a pond and when it became too large for that he placed it in a lake. Manu noticed that even when the fish grew huge, it remained pleasant to hold and easy to carry. Finally, the fish was so great in size that it could only be held in the arms of the wide ocean.

So Manu carried the fish all the way back to the shore of the great sea. He gave it back to the waters from which it had appeared. Upon being released, the fish spoke again and revealed to Manu that a great deluge was coming. It told him that everything solid would soon disappear in a wide flood, and that the great dissolution would purify all of existence. The fish advised Manu to prepare for the gathering flood and build a vessel that could ride on the wild seas and carry him to safety amidst the cleansing storms.

Of course Manu followed the advice of the fish and began building a large ship. Just as had been predicted, the flood-times came. As the waters began to roil and rise, the fish appeared again and spoke to Manu. The little fish had grown to huge proportions and it advised him to tie the ship to the great horn on its head. That being done, the fish pulled the ship across the raging seas until it reached a particular mountain peak that remained dry above the flooding waters.

Before departing, the fish revealed itself to be Vishnu, the original creator who dreamed life into existence while floating on the endless ocean of time. The fish asking for refuge was also a great deity. In helping the little fish survive, the human ancestor had lent a hand to the god of creation. Having assisted life in a small way, the original human received a great reprieve when the hard times and great dissolution came around.

Before departing, Vishnu taught Manu certain practices for keeping close to the breath of creation. When the flood waters receded Manu practiced what he had learned and found a secret that still remains part of life on earth. Manu found that the creation was ongoing and that he could participate in it. Although subject to great storms and threatening periods of change and dissolution, the ancestor of humanity was invited to participate in the energy and process of creation ongoing.

It's mostly forgotten in these days of overpopulation and growing ignorance, but sometimes it still turns out that a little help offered at the right time and in the right way can have a huge effect.

THE REALM OF THE FISHES

An old name for the great drama of devouring was the "realm of the fishes." The living oceans teem with huge fish feeding endlessly on smaller species. It happens day and night, year after year in great operas of devouring, in numbers that cannot be counted, much less understood. Life devours life and life grows from death at the basic levels of this world.

What happens in Nature is replicated in culture where every pond has its big fish and the small fry continually become the fodder for the big shots. Might tends to make right and the "powers that be" tend to claim whatever they desire. The greatest nations of the world consume the resources of the earth with reckless abandon. Call it the world of "dog eat dog," call it hard reality; it's there, a devouring level in every culture as well as a force throughout nature.

The realm of the fishes existed from the very beginning and remains part of the ongoing dynamic of creation and destruction that sustains life on earth. The basic conflicts and essential oppositions of life continue in the seas and jungles and plains of great Nature and also manifest throughout the cultures of the world. In Nature the conflicts and devourings happens automatically, quite naturally; in culture it happens both unconsciously and with willful intentions.

Arguments like that between adherents of one god and another or between evolution and creationism typically take place at the level of the realm of the fishes with each side trying to devour the other in order to become the big fish of the moment. Desiring to simply have it one way may win the day, but another day dawns and another big fish, the new big idea or the next world power shows up hungry with desire and ready to devour whatever delicacy happens to be nearby.

Yet there are also unusual occasions and exceptional times when things run "contra naturum" and seemingly against Nature. Nature goes against what seems most natural. A hidden aspect of life goes against the grain the way certain fish swim upstream no matter what. Something unexpected in Nature is able to go against natural law. An equally powerful, underlying theme of life goes against typical cultural patterns where an "underdog effect" can reverse matters and a small change can lead to a great effect. This world, it turns out, has more than one level; it includes evolving energies as well as creative moments.

The story of Manu and the fish depicts two strong forces, both present at the edge where the solid earth and the waves of change meet. Certainly, a devouring energy surges through the sea of life and big swallows small only to be eaten in turn by something larger than itself. Yet a contrary force occurs when a small change shifts the level of life and the storms of destruction become replaced by new waves of creation. Bigger devours smaller, yet a little change in awareness can make a great difference as well.

Like old Manu, humanity continues to stroll through the middle of existence, sometimes listening to the subtle voice that indicates how and where to be creative; at other times mindlessly devouring the resources of the earth and risking being devoured in turn. Fortunately, humans descend from "old hands" like Manu who found a way to enter the process of creation and become a little makeweight in the scales between time and eternity. Life on earth ever hangs in the balance and humanity plays a crucial part, that was settled a long time ago, back when things were just beginning. Either people learn to lend a hand to creation or else they tend to unconsciously swim in the realm of the fishes.

It's an important thing to know about, especially when the floods of change come and everything familiar seems about to be washed away. At certain times, in the great back and forth of the tides of creation and destruction, nature needs a little helping hand and culture needs to return to practices that assist the continuing song of creation.

Manu represents the sense that when a person becomes truly big they can learn to bow to something other than simple self-interest and can serve something beyond themselves. Humanity, if it awakens more fully to the creative ancestral prototype that sleeps within, can act contra naturum and go against blind needs and unconscious, selfish greed. Humanity remains capable of bending to the earth again and learning to assist the little fish of creation to find some refuge and ways to survive the great changes already underway.

Helping the "other," it turns out, secretly helps oneself. The act of genuinely serving something beyond and seemingly below oneself can have a hidden benefit. Saving that which seems helpless redeems the redeemer as well. A little help can be repaid tenfold. Of course, if the help is offered in hopes of a greater return, all bets are off. That's the realm of the fishes slipping back in. It may be human nature to make a deal in hopes of a good return; but it is contra naturum to sacrifice one's personal comfort and desires in order to redeem something in greater need.

The Sanskrit name for the realm of the fishes was *artha*, meaning the ground of conflict and competition, the fields of life where people struggle to achieve something recognizable and tangible in the world. Politics and war, business, and sports are arenas in which the energy of artha plays out in both competent and brutal ways. The opposite practice involved *dharma*, meaning the realm of duty and service, particularly service to family and to projects that benefit others and help insure that life and love will continue.

The old idea was that each person has a proportion of achievement to accomplish in one lifetime and each a share of service to be offered up. We live most fully when living out both energies in proportion to the shape of our innate soul. Thus, the wealthy have a duty to support the poor and those that handle power handle it best by placing it in service of something genuine beyond their own personal prestige.

With regard to the outer world, humans carry opposing energies, even conflicting interests. Sometimes achievement is required, sometimes selfless service. Sometimes reaching high, sometimes bending low. Little and big, high and low; those are part of the territory for the human psyche, part of the betwixt-and-between quality inherent in the soul.

Each person must live in a tension between opposing energies. Everyone must struggle with the issues of size, how big to be in a given situation; how little to require or request on another occasion. No one gets it completely right; everyone is a mixture of good and bad, just like the world around us.

Each person has a little self, an ego self that formed early on and presents itself as the true self on most occasions. The ego self always has some falseness in it because it formed partially to keep us from being devoured by life. The little self is necessary, even great Vishnu had to enter the world in a lesser form. Eventually, a person must ask for help and become a swimmer in greater and greater containers. It's the inner Self, the deep Self that has the capacity to grow larger and larger with genuine knowledge and practices that connect to the hidden forces of creation.

Sometimes the ego takes on the demeanor of a little fish in order to survive devouring aspects of the family or the community nearby. Later, that little self can cultivate a false humility so that the soul fails to grow. By staying small and unrealized the person survives, yet doesn't learn to contribute in meaningful ways.

Others survive by growing up too soon; they enter the grown-up world where dog eats dog early and later continue to insist on that reality. They persist on the paths of personal achievement long after any real value comes from their competitive efforts. They fail to find fulfillment even while surrounding themselves with grand houses and swollen accounts. Whatever helps one to adapt to life and survive the rough waters to begin with can one day become a danger to one's awakening and growth.

The bigger Self has a deep trust in life whereas the little self lives in fear of being over-looked or in terror of being swallowed up. Manu bent down when asked for help and acted from the big Self within. He found a sympathy that runs deep inside humanity, an age-old quality equal to the devouring energy of the realm of the fishes.

The really big fish is one in which the soul awakens to its dream of life. While in touch with that inner sense it has no need to devour others, but carries a compassion for the frailties of life and a sympathy for those in danger.

Acting from the big Self or the deep soul makes a person original, like Manu who lived close to the origins and was able to be of assistance to the endangered species as well as a servant to the god of creation. Manu turns out to be a friend of a god, and god turns out to be dwelling in little things that might be overlooked or dismissed as unworthy of our full attention.

It's like the famous occasion when someone asked a holy man why it was that no one saw god anymore. The world had come upon hard times and the horizon of life looked dark and troubled with storm clouds. People wondered whether god had become tired of the world and all the errors and mistakes of human societies.

The holy man didn't deliberate long before answering. No one saw god anymore because people were unwilling to bend low enough. People were looking in the wrong direction; they expected help from above when the redeeming energy was inside them and near those most threatened in the world. Since most had taken to relying on the religious experiences of others, they expected the divine to be high above this fallen world. Looking down to find something holy seemed patently unorthodox and possibly blasphemous.

Yet sometimes the higher elements must be sought in lowly places. By its very nature, the divine often goes against the grain. That which comes to be considered holy is often anything but orthodox to begin with. Manu and Noah and all the old thinkers that came to be considered the founders of orthodox attitudes were unorthodox to begin with. All the great makers and founders and pathfinders start out in contrary ways; it is that very quality that makes them unique and open to the sacred.

Not only that, but the holy ones find god right here on earth. Manu simply touched a fish, Noah turned a dream into a ship. Didn't Moses keep running into burning bushes? The divine hides in the things of the world causing the smallest entity to have some hidden divinity. It isn't that more people are needed who will follow the "letter of the law." That often causes more trouble than it cures, especially when the times demand some sort of surrender and an awareness of the suffering in this world. Usually, what's needed most are those who can lend a hand in creative ways, those who can sympathize with the plight of the lowly and become bigger than their usual self.

Many people prefer their god to be "holier than thou" and a confirmed resident of a much higher plane. The notion that god made the world and then departed for a higher place suits many people. They like the idea of a "deus absconditus;" a god who starts everything up only to abscond to a better place. That way things seem clearly divided with higher and lower firmly separated. Anything judged to be below them can also be dismissed for being god-less and forsaken. Lower things, lower people, even lower instincts can be condemned as unworthy of the sight of god.

The trouble with those who take such a one-sided approach is that they can only reach the divine when this world no longer exists. The heaven they wait for only appears after this fallen realm consumes itself. They see the worlds as sequential rather than interconnected. They miss the whispering of the divine in the presence of the fish of this moment even if they use an abstract fish as an emblem of the god they imagine to be in the higher realm.

As a god idea, Vishnu presents a continuous involvement of the divine in this world. Vishnu incarnated many times, often taking the form of an animal, although sometimes a lowly beggar boy. The deity can appear in any form because he secretly dwells at the center of each creature. In that world view everything remains connected to the divine realm, the world that remains behind and yet continues to be necessary to this world.

If the divine waits to be found nearby or within, then all those qualities relegated to heaven might be found right on earth. In that case this realm becomes more sacred and each being in it something to approach with greater respect. Yet such notions only appear where people become willing to bow to the reverence of life and bend low enough so that the heart can rise above the head with its fixed attitudes and strange need to be superior to other elements of creation.

CHAPTER 9

HIDDEN CONTINUITIES

In order for things in this world to change people might have to listen to little things, learn to hear again the language of nature and learn to trust the little voice that speaks from within. Noah had to follow the dream that awakened in him whether or not others understood his calling. Manu had to accept that little creatures have important needs and can communicate them. This immediate sense of the sacredness of all life appears in most religions; yet it becomes forgotten whenever the high doctrines and solemn dogmas claim to be the only fish in the ponds of spirit.

When the end seems near, little redemptions can shift the underlying patterns of both nature and culture. Seen this way, there's no need for this world to end. The divine, so longed for and sought after, has been hiding in the last place where most look for it. There's no need to believe in some great salvation if the divine can be found in nearby aspects of the incarnate world.

The notion that little saves big, that a small change can have a huge affect keeps being lost and rediscovered as the seas of time both wash things away and return them again to the shores of awareness. The tale of Manu and the little fish is one reminder of the immediate and immanent connections between things divine and the natural word.

In acting out of instinctive sympathy for the creatures of nature Manu doesn't simply survive the latest dangers, but also learns how to be part of creation ongoing. In rescuing a small and nearby aspect of life he enters the redemptive practices that don't so much save the world as allow it to grow while redeeming humanity a little.

The little fish that appeared to Manu was the first of a series of incarnations on the part of Vishnu. Each time the earthly realm becomes unbalanced and the struggle between life and death intensifies, the creator takes an earthly form and reenters creation. When the world seems old with worry, ancient ideas are also near and trying to become known again.

We are the descendants of old characters like Manu and Noah. We are the current inheritors of the dream of life and the mystery of creation. Our hands are never far from the core issues of life and the old practices for remaining creative and fully imaginative. That's more than most people want to know of life, so most pretend that creation happened back then and can't be found again until all this comes to an end. Old folk myths warn against such simple notions; like intelligent little fish they whisper that it's time to bend down and connect to the old ways of earth wisdom and the hidden Self within the self.

The old idea of the *atman* described the essence of the world as being both bigger than big and smaller than small. This sense of big and little also exists in the soul of each person, so that each person has an innate ability to resonate with the smaller than small and to imagine that which appears bigger than big. The old Greek thinkers called it the *cosmos*, from the root *cosm*, meaning order or form. Cosmos is the big picture, the whole thing seen as a whole, yet also a story that makes sense on all levels.

Macro is the old Greek root meaning "big or large." And combining "macro" and "cosm" creates the macrocosm, the highest order, the whole big thing, the bigger than big and larger than life sense of the undivided, unified universe. The macrocosm encompasses the largeness and largesse of the world, the universe with its universals; the whole whirling, singing, cosmic, metaphysical, mystical, mystifying, enchanted thing.

Cosmos is the natural order of things, the grand, over-all scheme and the underlying unity as well. It's the World, capitalized; the universe when seen as whole and integrated; the universal Oneness, once and for all. Yet, the macrocosm includes many microcosms, smaller versions of the cosmic order, even microscopic replicas of the whole big thing.

Micro means "little or tiny," the essential cosmic designs in diminutive form. Whereas the macrocosm presents the bigger than big, microcosms involve the smaller than small, the "mini-verses" and minute versions that also reflect the order and form of the greater universe. Macro and micro are secretly connected, they reflect each other; they interact in subtle and mysterious ways. "As above, so below," people used to say; "As it is in heaven, so also on earth."

Cosmology was the old study of the whole thing, the cosmic ligaments and the mythic narrations that considered it all at once. In cosmology, turn about is fair play. While it's evident that a big shift in the heavens can change everything on earth, it turns out that under certain circumstances a small shift can alter the whole thing as well. Micro changes can affect the macrocosm; as below so above and what happens deep within can become so throughout.

There is a hidden continuity in the world that sometimes reveals itself as in microphysics where a small change can be seen to have a big effect. In a sense, physics always verges upon becoming metaphysics again. The knock-on-wood physical world keeps slipping out of hand and hinting at cosmic schemes and universal designs. All genuine studies, including the hard sciences, verge upon encounters with the open secrets of the universe, where all things are revealed to be secretly connected and interacting despite differences in size and levels of being. Cosmology is revelation ongoing with the bigger than big and smaller than small interacting in surprising ways, sometimes seen through science, always being revealed by myth.

It turns out that even creation needs help once in a while. In holding the little fish Manu also handles the great whale it becomes over time. In bending low to the earth he finds the living breath of spirit. More often than not some small piece of knowledge becomes necessary if the whole thing would change. At that point the human spirit can become the makeweight that shifts things towards creation again.

In this world things appear doubled, big and small, left and right, inside and out, high and low. Similarly there are two ongoing stories, each weaving ways through the wonders and disasters of life, the cosmic tale of the whole world and the intricate stories that can only be lived through particular lives. Both tales are told simultaneously, concurrently; meeting at certain points and conversing in subtle ways. Each is a grand experiment, each a mystery revealing itself to itself; eternity continuing to speak through the visible world and through each living being.

We are part of that great telling whether we know it or not; each person a story the soul of the world tells in the continuous conversation between beginning and ending, in the middle waters, between life and death. One long story needing to be lived out again and again and never lived the same way twice. We inherit the ongoing story as well as the ongoing disasters that occur within it.

When the story of the world wants to explore endings and find some new beginnings, people are plagued with last thoughts and fears of finality. The End seems close at hand and we feel unable to handle it. Everything moves faster and faster, like a rushing tide. There seems to be no time left and no way to change the course set for disaster. Yet fears that everything is coming apart, that this is The End, are part of the continuing tale of the world. All told before, convincingly too; with storms and desperate people and animals being lost.

OLD NOAH AGAIN

When news of The End came to Noah he understood the nature of the work to do. The dream of the deluge awakened something already in him. He began building bigger things. Inside the news that The End was coming were instructions for beginning again. It wasn't just that he gathered pairs of animals and became a savior. There was a thread joining those pairs to begin with; there was a dream waiting to awaken in him. Inside the ark there was a living covenant; subtle threads and lifelines that held one level of life together with others.

Only those convinced by their own dreams can see the hidden designs behind the troubles of the world. To the common eye Noah looked particularly foolish. Yet he would have been foolish in a worse way had he refused the inner project. Who can explain this to those whose eyes have not yet opened to their own inward seas?

These aren't religious stories intended to teach moral lessons or substantiate abstract rules, rather they are tales that try to recall the nature of the cosmos. The old flood stories don't persist in order to inform us what happened before, but to remind us of the project we came here to undertake now. The dream came and Noah got hired to do eccentric things. Animals began to long for faraway places, water dissolved familiar shorelines. The certainty of life began to slip away. Those who held anything too tightly were unable to shift when the tide changed. The problem wasn't that the end of the world had come; rather the issue was how to act when it seemed that way.

When The End seems near old ideas return in order to be known again. Subtle voices hint at unseen designs. If we begin listening as Manu did, as old Noah did, we become gainfully employed and find the exact projects and practices needed to keep things afloat for a long time to come. Secretly, each of us is a Noah sent on a distinct and seemingly foolish errand that can help the world as well as fulfill us. If we listen, we add to the story of life; if not, we join those who become foolish in the wrong way.

Our job isn't to comprehend everything, but to learn which story we are in. Our job is to be like Noah, find the thread of our own dream and live it all the way to the end. Our job is to be fully alive in the life we have; to pick up the invisible thread of our own story and follow where it leads. In order to be fully alive we have to be a little foolish, a little bit listening to some god, a little bit hanging out with the animals.

Some people actually try to reproduce the old ark, try to trace the route it sailed, try to take a moral lesson from it only to miss the essential sense that it was a dream that awakened Noah. He was a dreamer, not a literalist. He had a sense for animals and feeling for long voyages. His dream took him far from the mainstream; it set him on a course that left all certainty behind. Noah's boat was too crowded with life and too foolish with dreams to simply sink.

People easily forget how the great seers lived outside contemporary beliefs and beyond the understanding of the local religions. Later, lesser religious thinkers claim the actions of those knowers as proof of their own beliefs. Few of them actually set sail or test the waters of their own dreams. Few of them negotiate designs with unseen deities and wind up with something that really floats. What causes people to drown in the sea of changes is fixed beliefs, abstract ideologies, and the fear of letting go of familiar things.

When there's water everywhere nothing can remain certain. Any excess of certainty sinks the boat. Noah had no anchor, theological or otherwise. What good is an anchor when water is everywhere? When the floods of change come, rigid ideas and fixed beliefs may look like life rings, but in the long run it's better to learn how to sail or even to swim.

These are Noah times. Whole species disappear each day, languages go mute, forests fall heavily and people increasingly forget who they are before they die. It's a time of loss, a period of great atrocities, an epoch rampant with refugees. We are forced to look at the ways in which things end and disappear. Everyone becomes a refugee when life changes so rapidly, so tragically, so inexplicably.

Noah was a refugee as well; his only passport, the dreams that carried him. We are all children of Noah, shipmates with all the animals, dreamers on the ocean of time. We float on great tides of living and dying, blown on by the winds of eternity, looking out for a place to settle and continue the story of life. Our job is to be fully alive in the life we have and being fully alive means being a little foolish and open to unseen things.

Meaningful projects wait to awaken inside people. Most dwell near the essential tasks of their lives and only seem far from that work because of the distractions of the realm of the fishes and the fears of the little self.

Manu, representing humankind, held Vishnu, the god of creation, in his hand without even being aware of it. His instinctive reverence for life and willingness to serve crossed boundaries that typically separate species from species and nature from spirit. That's what old Noah was doing with the parade of animals into the ark. It wasn't a "genome project," nor was he simply and dutifully following orders. Noah had the same sense of extending sympathy across boundaries and finding compassion for the shared anguish of living creatures.

In the dark times, when creation and destruction appear with each wave of change, the issue isn't simply to find a fixed belief or a great cause to become consumed with. Rather, the idea involves becoming like Manu who heard the subtle, nearby cry and bent to offer assistance. What calls to us also calls from within; what needs attention resides in the inner seas as well.

In some stories the fish asking for help appears as golden. Either a golden fish rising from the depths of the sea before some poor fisherman or a fish with a gold ring hidden inside. There's a message in this discovery of gold from the depths. These stories are not just about the outside world. Something swims within the soul waiting to be heard and become known. Something deep and valuable remains hidden within each person; it desires to be recognized and held in awareness and cared for. Though small and subtle to begin with, the golden self can grow to surprising proportions. This golden self tends to appear when times are hard and existence itself feels threatened.

We are the direct and indirect descendants of old Manu who knew when to bend low and what to raise up. We are the grandchildren of Old Noah who survives inside the waters of human imagination and continues to design projects and dream on the inwards seas. If we settle for a statistical world view and a literal view of life we will lose the subtle connections to those dreams and find ourselves on the wrong errand in life.

ENTER THE SCHOLAR

It's like the scholar who was sailing from one place to another and of course carrying his load of heavy books. Finding himself at the shore of a great ocean he sought a ship in order to travel across it. After finding a suitable vessel the scholar wanted to know who was in charge of the crossing. He was a man of questions and answers and he wanted to know what was what.

Upon boarding the ship he asked if the captain was familiar with the ideas of philosophy, the issues of evolution, and the arguments of the theologians. The man of the sea had to admit he hadn't read any of these subjects and wasn't schooled in the latest theories. The scholar informed him that without such knowledge he had wasted most of his life.

At any rate, the course had been charted and the ship had to set sail. When the vessel reached the open seas a wild storm blew up, the skies became dark and the waters grew rough. When the gale didn't abate, but grew more treacherous moment to moment, the captain went to check on the scholar. He asked if in the course of his studies the leanred man had learned to swim. The man of books and fine ideas said he had never taken the time to learn swimming or any other exercise. "Then all of your life has been wasted," said the captain, "for this ship is going down."

When The End seems near, it's important to know how to swim in the rough waters of life. Here, swimming means being deep in the inner story, being buoyant with the work we came here to do and finding practices that serve the life of the soul as well as the life of the mind. The problem with the scholar wasn't that he was an intellectual; the problem was that the ideas he carried couldn't keep him afloat in the seas of change. The issue wasn't that he took religious issues seriously, but that he believed more in the word written down than in living practices. Books are a wonderful thing, but a little heavy and obtuse when immediate knowledge of the world becomes necessary.

In this life the sinking feeling is never far away. Sometimes we have to abandon all designs and jump into the waters of life and swim with all our instincts. In the moment of jumping overboard, everything seems lost and we do die in some fashion. Yet as we try to swim, something old and resourceful awakens in us.

Whenever we can recall what is threaded through us, life's bigger designs appear again. Then, we are carried on by the winds of the world. Of course, most forget the specific message and everyone drowns a few times before learning to swim. The trick is to learn what really carries us when the seas get rough; what has secretly carried us all along.

The big, codified stories with their weighty texts and attendant institutions eventually become dry, fatally cracked, and unable to funnel the waters of life to the common folk. Yet, the waters of life don't simply disappear. When the robberies of time diminish the orthodox notions and fixed ideas, folk myths and wisdom tales whisper to the edges of the mind. The old stories continue, no matter what; they pull threads of eternity through the loops of history.

When the fixed doctrines and grand dogmas begin to unravel and the end of their swollen sway seems near, the waters of life flow back into the streams and rivulets of folk lore and folk myth that have provided guidance and sustenance for the souls of folk for millennia. When the surface of the world quakes in ways that threaten the halls of culture and even the persistent cycles of nature, the waters of genuine knowledge and healing flow into the smaller containers which include the little stories of the folk traditions, the age-old folkways, the alternative vessels of healing, and the big dreams that common people have.

Living myths and folk tales attend to intermediate, in-between spaces and places, the betwixt-and-betweens where the loose threads and remainders of existence wait to be found again and woven back into life.

Myths and stories fill the spaces between one thing and another, between one epoch and the next, between one civilization and another, between one religion and the others. In the long run, what matters is an awakening of the Old Mind, the story mind that recalls how to survive the great sea changes that eradicate all that people deem to be so solid and important.

There are troubles that eat at the roots of creation, occasions when what troubles this world also troubles the otherworld. This realm needs the ongoing touch of god and the otherworld benefits when those in this realm overcome the little self. Each helps the other and in proper proportion. The human hand, far too small to handle the great tides and times of radical change, can be just big enough to rescue a little life when the devouring forces of the earth fall out of balance with creation.

Something within the human soul is immeasurable, tied to the eternal. Our need to dream proves it; so does our sense of longing. We arrive with eyes of vision, soft and subtle those eyes, wrapped in dreams, used to floating on inner seas. If we don't learn to see in that way again, we drift through the world, lacking purpose, despairing of finding meaning, or else pretending to certainties like the scholars and clerics who sink in the end below the surprising currents of life.

Whatever the reason for the dissolution, be it the wide-ranging cycles of Great Nature, the reaction of the gods to the impious behavior of the majority of folks, the recklessness of technology, or the flood of people over populating the swollen earth, be it any of these or all of the above, the point of reckoning in the flood tales involves individual human capacity to catch wind of the shape and meaning of their own lives and learning to swim in the great sea of existence.

CHAPTER 10

THE FIRST PILGRIMAGE

In this world people wander in all directions, sometimes driven by simple curiosity, sometimes running from the past. People wander about and wonder along and sometimes feel the desire to make a pilgrimage to find greater meaning, to be near some holy place, or approach some beloved presence. Every journey must begin with the first step and some say that a sage named Markandeya took the initial step on a pilgrimage from which all subsequent journeys proceed.

Markandeya was another of those progenitors that appeared when things were just starting out. The one who came to be revered as a great sage began his journey while the world was being dreamed up by the god Vishnu. Inside that wondrous dream the first wanderer became awed by the beauty of the world and he instinctively began the practice of making pilgrimages from one place to another.

Surrounded by beauty and inclined towards devotion, the sage wandered along on the first great walkabout. Along the way he somehow slipped off the path; maybe that explains why so many who take up a spiritual path come to fall from grace even now.

When that first pilgrim slipped up he fell into the bottomless, timeless sea that surrounded everything at that time. If he hadn't learned how to swim in those eternal currents, he would have been completely lost. And if Vishnu hadn't had a hand in it, Markandeya might have drowned out of sheer hopelessness and despair. Sometimes the helping hand comes from the human side of life, sometimes it has to come from the eternal realm nearby.

Being a god of creation, Vishnu had a natural affinity for water and for animals that dwell in the waters. He appeared to old Manu as a fish in the treacherous seas of life, but was first described as resting on the infinite coils of a serpent that floated on the cosmic sea. The god reclined in comfort on the expansive waters while meditating and sleeping and dreaming up the entire world. Most gods have many names and one of his was Narayana, the "one who moves the waters" and in so doing moves all of life.

The great serpent that figures in so many creation tales also has many names; one was Ananta, meaning "endless." Yet the serpent also could be addressed as Vishnu. The limitless ocean could be called Vishnu as well, for the blue-skinned god was the source of everything substantial and insubstantial. Vishnu was sleeping and dreaming away while resting on the coils of Vishnu who floated upon Vishnu as well.

The three aspects present at the beginning were distinct, yet also a unity. They depict three essential elements of the dream of this world: the giant figure of a deity in humanlike shape, the serpent of endless coils and countless forms, and the formless ocean of night that surrounds everything that exists. All were there at the beginning and each an aspect of Vishnu, the one who moves the waters of eternity and dreams the dream of life.

Within the dreaming god all the vibrant terrains of the earth existed in elemental beauty. And within those pristine landscapes the first ancestor wandered about and enacted the original pilgrimage from which all the wanderings of humanity have come. The original seeker saw each earthly place with fresh eyes, saw them as part of a living network of natural shrines and wonders.

Instinctively, he bowed to the beauty of the world and worshiped at each place in a generous, easy way, enacting the ideal role of the human devotee doing the natural work of exploring the world and reflecting upon the wonder of creation. The old pilgrim saw the earth as it appeared in the cosmic dream. All was fine with Markandeya and with the world.

Then, for some unexplained reason, the first little slip-up happened, the first mistake, and first hint of a nightmare in the dream of the world. Despite the ideal conditions and the assumed good intentions, Markandeya stumbled and fell off the path. It was the first slip, a primal pratfall, the original loss of grace and some say that we have been falling ever since.

To make matters worse, great Vishnu was sleeping with his mouth open; more than that, the god was snoring. Everything at the beginning, they say and even snoring, had to start somewhere. Vishnu slept with his mouth open and snored away while dreaming up the dream of life. The dreaming god made a deep, sonorous sound amidst the endless silence of the limitless ocean of existence. Then, inadvertently, accidentally and unexpectedly the first seeker slipped and tumbled right out of the mouth of the all-containing god.

Mortally astonished, the original saint dropped from the tongue of god and landed in the cosmic sea. Ever since, people experience a sinking feeling in the pit of the stomach whenever something starts to go seriously awry. Whether it be an unintended slip of the tongue or an unintentional loss of the way, each soul that enters the dream of life repeats and continues that original slip. All falling began then, including falling out of love and failing in one's devotions.

Maybe it was bound to happen. The first holy person became accidentally voided by the sleeping, snoring god and there was nowhere to fall except into the void. The first person to lay eyes on the wonders and beatitudes of creation was also the first to look straight into the emptiness of the void. As an idea, it was the void; as an image, it was the primal sea. In the beginning, ideas and images were entwined; as time moved on, it became harder to hold the two things together, the image and the idea; the dream of life and its origin in the void.

Markandeya fell into nothing and he fell into the wine-dark sea. He drifted amidst dark waters, blind and unknowing in the starless expanse of an endless night. He became completely disoriented and plagued with doubts and questions. He knew the world to be a harmonious and beautiful place, but where were the moon and stars that wrote stories on the sky? Where the sun that taught each day to see? Where the determined stands of mountains and the terra firma of the earth? Even the wind that promised change was absent now.

He was adrift in the emptiness and awash in a growing uncertainty. Cast upon the limitless waters and alone in the unrelenting obscurity, he pondered in fear. All that he had known before seemed impossible now, everything but a mirage, all an empty illusion. Was he even alive, had he ever been? Was this all a dream? Had it been a dream before? Which the real, which the unreality: the endless void or the well-shaped world that he once walked within?

Markandeya began to drown in despair and suffocate in a fear that seemed to chase his life through the narrow shapes of his bones. Each direction appeared empty, each hope a quick despair. He was exiled from god and from the earth and felt overexposed in all his parts. Being unable to see anything beyond himself, he was forced to draw any sense of being from within himself or else sink heavily into the blind sea.

Suddenly, Markandeya became aware of a vague shape somewhere beyond wherever he was. There seemed to be something partly submerged in the expanse of water. It appeared as a mountain range vaguely breaking the dark horizon in the distance. And it seemed to glow from a radiance within itself. Filled with amazement and feeling an inner glimmer of hope, the sage began to swim towards the glowing shape.

As he drew closer to the apparition, he became flooded with joy as his eyes began to realize that the shape in the void was the immense form of the sleeping god. Now, the solitary saint was swimming mightily and swimming towards god. Moved by renewed awe, he opened his lips to ask aloud who or what was before him. As he formed the words to speak, a giant hand seized him up and he was swallowed back.

Markandeya, wet with doubts and still dripping with some despair, found himself once again wandering a path within the surprising dream of the earth. Although back on familiar ground, the saint was a bit unsteady. His experience of the void stuck to him, being unforgettable and deeply lodged within, even as he looked again upon the beauty of the earthly landscapes before him.

He had seen the void, had tasted it, been right in it. He had seen the form of god, a giant shape, manlike or womanlike, so huge it was hard to tell. He had glimpsed the deity, yet could not comprehend it. Now, he wandered within that which he could not comprehend. He had seen the other side of existence and part of him felt a great distance from anything created. He had felt the warm breath of god and the penetrating chill of the void. He remembered both, but understood neither. Which was real and which the dream?

Back in the dream of life, he found himself dripping wet with the nether waters. He was saved, redeemed, yet disoriented again. This time the seeker was disoriented to the dream of life. And the memory of an ocean of emptiness lingered in the waking world. He found himself carrying on the questioning that had begun in the great sea of doubts.

Although he could feel the path beneath his feet, he knew he could slip at any moment and fall out of the grace of the dream of the world. Now, he pondered and prayed his way carefully along. He noticed the silence between the notes of birdsongs; he felt the distance between stars and at times knew a gnawing emptiness within. How slight the veil between things could be, and how close the hand of god!

Markandeya had to consider that he lived a dream within a dream and lived within a questioning that doubted all that exists. He had tasted of the absence of things and knew in some inexplicable way that all and nothing were both nearby and within him as well.

And we, who come along so long after the dreaming up and fashioning of the world, are the descendants of that pondering pilgrim. We are the latest wanderers in the dream of god and the most recent inheritors of the fall into obscurity. We sleep inside the dream of the world and can't help but sometimes worry that we might wind up in the great void.

Is this world reality or all an illusion? People ask this when struck down by disasters or stricken with doubts. Myths tend to answer: Yes. It's all there and not there, like the breath within the breath, like the No hidden within each Yes and the Yes secreted behind every No. Does what happens in the world matter or not? The answer again: Yes. Those who think the whole thing to be a simple illusion fail to realize that it is the great illusion, the illusion that is both reality and a dream.

In the Hindu mythos, water represents the primary materialization and life-maintaining essence. One name for that essence was *maya*. Lord of Maya was another of the many names of Vishnu. In the West maya has often been translated to mean "just an illusion," a simple trick that people can escape or extricate themselves from. Yet Maya is a tricky word; on one hand it means "magic," a kind of cosmic sleight of hand. On the other hand it means "matter." Maya involves the great trick of existence, the grand illusion of life that contains and sustains everything that matters in this world. The material world bubbles up continually from the void.

As the magic of life maya circulates through the world in the form of essential fluids, as rain and sap, as semen and milk, as honey and oil, and blood. These various "waters of life" are the magical substances that carry the generative and renewable powers of the original matter, the maya of the dream of the world.

It may all be an illusion, but it's the necessary illusion and any who find a genuine path and way to be in life must begin with what matters most to them. Maya is the stuff of dreams amidst the dreams of stuff, the magic of life and love amidst the mundane, material world. Magic means change and maya means the capacity to change midstream and transform in the midst of the magical exchange between the incarnated world and the waters of nonbeing.

Like Markendeya, we fall in and out of the dream of this world. In the modern world a person can go a long time with no hints of god on the horizon. It can become difficult to remember the honesty of standing before a natural wonder and learning to fully bow.

These days, it's hard not to feel the presence of the void nearby. Part of the experience of being in the modern world seems to be the awareness of losing the world altogether. To be modern seems to involve falling from the mouth of god and feeling the chill of emptiness nearby, even awakening in a terror that the dream of the world might end altogether. It's like the dread feelings that can arise when a new report depicts how the polar ices caps might melt away in the heat of global warming and flood the earth. Maybe catastrophes are required in order to find proper devotions again.

Each person is a pilgrim in the dream of god and each slips in predictable and surprising ways. How else could it be? We ride on the breath of the god and usually fail to know it until we fall from grace. Call it losing the way, call it unconsciousness, inner emptiness; call it cynicism, nihilism, double depression; call it being lost and feeling next to nothing.

Mankind has always been soaked with divine imagination and wet with fears of emptiness, absence, and abandonment. The all and nothing of this world has always been whispering at the edges of human awareness. Now, the ancient questions and existential issues appear in regular news reports of impending planetary disasters and threats from nihilistic terrorists.

The dream of life and the threat of annihilation; the abundant wonders of nature and the presence of the void have moved closer together and seem to call for attention. The modern world has reached a crossroads that older cultures have encountered many times before. Old philosophies and practices for handling the dilemmas of existence and the tension of the opposites have existed for thousands of years. And interest in traditional philosophies and tribal practices has been growing rapidly in the West.

THE TENSION OF THE OPPOSITES

This old tale and others like it were told throughout the ancient Far East to those who desired to become a "yogi," a sage or spiritual seeker. *Yogi* and *yoga* come from old roots that mean "to yoke," "to unite;" particularly to yoke oneself to the divine. Yoga can mean any path or practice that sustains a union between the individual soul and the source of life. Markandeya was doing yoga once he started swimming towards god.

The purpose of yogic practices involves the making of genuine individuals. *Individual* means "un-divided," the one not divided on the inside and thus able to withstand great pressures from the outside world. The genuine individual or undivided person must be made again and again from creative tension generated by facing fundamental oppositions within the self.

Becoming a genuine individual requires learning the oppositions within oneself. Those who fail or refuse to face the oppositions within themselves have no choice but to find enemies to project upon. *Enemy* simply means a "not-friend;" unless a person deals with the not-friend within they require enemies around them.

In critical moments in the lives of individuals and communities the basic elements and energies of life polarize. What first appears as a small error, a little slip off the path, an accident that no one could foresee, grows into a full-blown dilemma. Soon, we feel torn apart, thrown back and forth between opposing moods and conflicting attitudes. It seems that a choice must be made, yet choosing either side seems disastrous.

We become crucified by irreconcilable aspects of a conflict that in truth was there all along. Choose one side of a dilemma and the other side resurfaces with a vengeance. For picking one side or being "one-sided" about a true dilemma only delays and even intensifies the issue. Choose one side and the conflict will return at a deeper level at some future time. That's the nature of the genuine dilemmas of life in this left and right, dark and light, abundant and empty world.

Only when a person can experience both sides simultaneously and hold the tension does a third thing appear that allows a genuine creative solution. And only a creative solution can bring a genuine resolution and avoid the threat of dissolution.

Genuine change and meaningful transformation are the secret aims of the tension inside life itself. If a person or a culture chooses one side of a dilemma too soon the hidden third or underlying unity fails to appear and the dilemma deepens and leans towards the edges of the abyss. Many wars begin because those in power fail to hold the tension of the opposites. Huge projects collapse and turn to dust because those involved lack personal and collective ways of holding the tension long enough for a creative solution to appear.

In the great exchange of the modern market of information some of the practices of yoga have wandered over into the busy streets of the modern mass societies of the West. It's as if an instinct for yoking has awakened and an intuition for a greater maturity has surfaced. Maturity, they used to say, involves a greater and greater capacity to withstand and understand the tension of the opposites.

Whereas literalists and fundamentalists tend to choose one pole of any dilemma or opposition; whereas modern political parties tend towards demonizing each other; the creative individual and genuine solutions are born of enduring the tension between opposing poles. A certain relief can come in removing oneself from the tension of knowing and not-knowing, of being and not-being. Yet the refusal to bear the weight of living, the gravity of awareness and the necessary burdens of the soul can eventually drain vital energy and lead to a loss of freedom in life.

When people refuse to suffer the tension of the opposites in honest and artful ways, the uniqueness of life and the meaning of experience become obscured and repeatedly replaced by endless skirmishes between opposing elements. Only when the tension of opposing forces can be held long enough does a genuine solution appear that can dissolve the tension and renew the flow of life at another level.

Genuine solutions only appear where dissolution is risked. Staying in the tension long enough generates something that was there but could not be seen. In the midst of the great tension Markandeya felt while in the darkness of the cosmic sea he began to see anew. Where there seemed to be nothing he caught site of the radiance of god, but first had to find some life resources within himself.

In falling out of the dream of life Markandeya had a life-changing experience. He found himself in an existential condition, having to face the great opposition between the abundant dream of life and the endless void. He who first found himself happily within the dream of the world had later to find the dream of the world within himself. In order to do that he had to face inner fears and layers of despair. He had to swim within his own oblivion in the existential version of sink or swim.

In order to orient himself back to the horizon of the divine the old sage had to find the dream within and the way he was meant to swim in the troubled waters that surround this world. In order to get his feet back on the ground he had to learn to swim with the force of his own unique life dream. Learning how we each are supposed to swim in the great waters of oblivion—that's the point when the world seems threatened and things seem about to fall into the abyss.

In learning to swim some sinking and fears of drowning are required. Any true awakening implies both commitments and letting something go. A person can't swim and hold on at the same time. Swimming is a form of surrender that requires trusting the waters we find ourselves in and letting go of all prior beliefs. It becomes easier to swim and aim for the divine horizon once the full implications of drowning have been accepted.

There are endless ways to swim and catch glimpses of god. When the time for spiritual swimming comes, any sighting of god is a godsend and anything that keeps one afloat becomes an act of devotion. In the sudden devotion of swimming for one's life there's precious little time to argue about the shape of god. That's the business of the scholars and clerics, many of whom prefer the dry ravines where the deities were said to have visited, but where the living waters of the divine no longer flow.

SWIMMING TOWARDS GOD

Swimming in god's ocean means accepting the waters of one's life and learning to trust the vague shape on the horizon of one's present knowledge. In this emotional, spiritual swimming, accuracy counts less than a willingness to brave the waters of uncertainty. When it comes to dreams and oblivion don't be like the scholar who disdained swimming when all the texts indicate that god made the waters first.

Why be like the learned man who lamented on his deathbed that all the fixed ideas and beliefs as well as the intellectual assumptions were of no use in the end? He learned too late that he had wasted much of his time. Yet even he learned in the last moment. Better to realize things sooner than that.

When the waters of the void are near it's the living dream within that gives buoyancy and makes the devotion of swimming possible. When the real swimming starts, all arguments are with god. As a word, god has roots like any other word. It comes from the Gothic *ghuth* and the Indo-European *ghut—ghuto* meaning: to implore. God is who or what we implore when all seems lost and there's nowhere else to turn.

Seen the other way around, each soul is secretly pulled by god; just as the divine hand was waiting once the old sage saw things more clearly and learned a way to swim amidst the uncertainty of life. People are secretly pulled towards one god or another. Yet each needs a practice, a way of swimming inside life in order to move in the right direction. Amidst the flood of changes and the threats of annihilation a genuine art or practice helps to keep the fears and doubts and the void at bay.

A practice helps bring the glowing shape of the dream of life into view again and again. For some, it's the waters of the great religions; others swim in unorthodox ways. There are many forms of practice; anything that moves one closer to genuine presence is a way. Whatever keeps one swimming in this ocean of god is a magnet that pulls the secret self up to the surface where consciousness can grow. No one except god fully notices our spiritual style and the secret persistence we bring to our lives.

A practice is like entering the void repeatedly and learning to swim again and again. The waters of practice have no beginning and no end. In a genuine practice, our head goes under the waters many times. Sometimes we feel the hand of the divine and sometimes the chill of the void. Empty and full, chaos and cosmos dancing back and forth across the hand of god. Such practices help to stir the old dream within us; the memory of a world made of sacred places and divine beauty. Lose that sense of divine purpose and we lose the world even if we succeed in more obvious ways.

We are made of the stuff of dreams and of nightmares, tossed back and forth on the breath of the gods. We live in two worlds, subjects of both visions. Awakening means knowing something of each, learning the song we carry within and facing the traumas handed to us as well. Awakening involves learning to swim in the waters of life.

The underlying meaning of maya involves the ability to hold opposing energies together. Notions of maya point to a secret union of the opposites, abundance and emptiness, dark and light, matter and spirit, old and young, endings and beginnings. Markandeya had been initiated into a knowledge of the maya or magic of great Vishnu, the god of creation. He had been fully exposed to the dream of the world as seen within the god and been dipped in the waters of oblivion. He became the model for the wise elder and sage who could tolerate great tensions and find yogic unity where others simply felt torn apart.

Many years passed inside the dream of the earth before a similar fall happened. Inexplicably, the old sage slipped again and found himself falling from the mouth of god only to be deposited back in the endless sea. This time he adjusted more quickly and held to the dream within himself. In short order he spotted an island nearby with a fig tree upon it and standing beneath the tree a luminous child cheerfully at play.

As he approached the island the youngster spoke and welcomed the old sage by name, saying: "Do not be afraid my child, but come closer here to me." The ageless holy man felt insulted by being called a child by a child. Child indeed! Who was more venerable and wise with age than the first pilgrim of this world? Didn't Markandeya mean the "undying one"? Even the gods referred to him as the Long-lived One.

"Who are you to call me a child?" asked the offended saint, forgetting all the ins and outs of the existential issues of the void. The little one answered, "I am your parent, the one who secretly sustains your life. I have a thousand heads. I am the cycle of the year that begins everything and takes it all away as well. I am the divine dreamer and the fount of wisdom. My name is birth and I am called death as well."

Markandeya suddenly understood that the ancient child before him was Vishnu showing him the contradictory aspects of evolution and dissolution, showing him the maya and magic of the deity that both creates and destroys, that sustains and annihilates. Suddenly, he felt great gratitude and privilege to receive such a direct revelation. Then, just as suddenly as he appeared, the divine child disappeared and the hand of Vishnu snatched up the holy man up and he was swallowed back again.

Inside the dreaming body of the divine, the sage felt a new level of gratitude and a new wave of wonder. This time instead of taking up his wandering habits again he sought a solitary place in which to rest and contemplate. After sitting quietly for a long time, he began to hear the breath of the dreaming god flowing out into the world and drawing back into the dream again. He realized that it was the life breath of the universe and that he was held in that breath even as he breathed his own life.

The old holy man attended carefully to this awareness of the breath of the universe. He made an art of that attention and that gave birth to the practice of "pranyama," which means to extend the breath and extend the vital force of life. The old sage took up the essential practice of participating in the breath of creation and extending the vital force of life. The indrawn breath he called "ham," the exhalation he termed "sa." Taken together they make up the in and out, the inspiration and the expiration, the endless breath of the universe.

The two breaths make up the world and also intone the name Hamsa, meaning a wild gander. Of course, Hamsa turns out to be another title of Vishnu who sometimes appears as a wild bird whose wings stir the breath of the world. Vishnu's choice of birds is no accident, for the wild gander can float easily on the surface of the ocean or suddenly lift its wide wings and begin a great migration, a grand pilgrimage to unseen places.

As emblem of the dual nature of creation the wild bird wanders between the two worlds, at home in the celestial heights as well as on the waters of existence. And we, who inherit the dream of the world with its landscapes of pristine beauty and the need to wander and wonder within it, are also residents in two realms. We follow the old knowers even when we know nothing of them. Whether conscious of it or not, our own breathing goes in and out and sings "ham" and "sa" and contributes to the enduring breath of life.

There is one more secret hidden in the tale of the old sage who fell from the mouth of god. As Markandeya listened to the song of the breath of life both within himself and in the universe, he began to hear it the other way around. At first it seemed but a mistake, another slip up and loss of continuity as had happened many time before.

Then the old saint caught onto the little joke, for "sa" and "ham" can also be translated as "this" and "I." When heard the other way around sa-ham, sa-ham can mean: this I am, this I am. The old pilgrim found himself breathing along with the dream of the world and riding on the endless ocean of the great void while breathing in and out and singing along: this I am, this I am. As above, so below, they used to say when people paid more careful attention to both the inner breath and the atmosphere that we breathe.

CHAPTER 11

COSM AND CHASM,
BEGINNING AND END

S ome old stories describe how the god Vishnu would take flight in
the form of a wild gander and soar into the upper realms. As the
cosmic bird took wing and flew high above it sang the song of existence
while looking down on the face of creation. As it flew farther and farther
away it rose into the eternal night taking the breath of the universe away.

At that moment, they say, the whole world drifts towards the chaos that
preceded creation. The breath of the deity withdraws from the myriad forms
of life and everything shifts back towards the original state of the primal,
endless ocean until the god dreams again and breathes the world back into
existence. The process takes hundreds of thousands of years, as if to imply
that the point is more cosmological story than literal accounting.

Cosmology involves all the images and ideas that people have found
throughout time to describe the origins as well as the dissolution of the
universe. Cosmology is a big deal, the study of big ideas, the universal
overviews and grand designs, the whole thing seen as a whole with each
thing having a place within it. Cosmology is storytelling on a grand
and grandiose scale, a mythologizing that attempts to make sense of the
enormity of the universe and the mystery of being in it.

Playing the human part in the great story involves trying to hold a vision of the whole thing. For people are naturally cosmological, unable to stop trying to imagine the entire world, top to bottom, how it all began, if it will ever end, and what role we play in the unfolding of it. Folk tales and little myths keep close to the ground and depend upon the wisdom of the earth; but cosmological stories are also a necessity and an essential way in which humanity expresses the hidden unity of the soul. Humans are the only cosmologists.

Cosmos means order, from the old Greek word *kosmein*, which gives "cosm" and "cosmopolitan." The outline of ancient cities often repeated a cosmological design, so that being at the center of the city also meant being at the center of the universe. That sense of being at the center made a person cosmopolitan. Primordial thought naturally places humans in the middle of the cosmic order, an essential link in the story-chain of being, destined to play a central role in the great drama of the world.

Cosmos also means the proper arrangement and placement of things, especially the grand composition, the "opus magnus" that includes the song of the spheres and the waves of cosmic harmony that flow throughout the universe. Each thing in its natural place, sustaining the song of the universe and everything imbued with hidden meaning; that's the cosmos.

The further we are from stories that make some sense of the whole thing, the more lost and confused we tend to become. Without a felt sense of cosmology people begin to feel accidental, lost in space, abandoned in the middle of nowhere. Without a working cosmology and a regenerative mythology, life can lose its sense of purpose causing the inevitable struggles of existence to seem random and pointless. When the sense of cosmological order and the center of life goes missing everything can turn darkly chaotic.

Pure chaos is the polar opposite of the great cosmic arrangement. Chaos comprises all that's confusing and disorderly and confounding in the world. The old Greek word *khaos* means "chasm" or "gaping void." Chaos is the abysmal abyss, the original rent in the world, the black hole from which things appear and into which they can disappear.

Chaos is the primal emptiness, the ever-present chasm, the endless night from which cosmos arose that threatens to swallow it all back again. Chaos connotes collapse, disorder, disorientation, fragmentation, things slipping away and falling apart; emptiness growing and the void becoming unavoidable. The chasm of chaos is filled with Nothing. It's the presence of absence, the absence of presence; it's the loss of all forms, the lack of any meaning, the nullity and nihilism vaguely waiting at the edge of all that seems certain and solid and established in the world.

Chaos slithers snakelike at the feet of all the marching orders of life and nips nightly at the edges of all that cosmos orders up and arranges. Chaos is the absence of forms and formalities; it includes all the bottomless pits and the lost causes, the nightmares that won't relent and the apocalyptic visions of annihilation that keep returning whenever things become uncertain. Call it dark matter, antimatter, a black hole. It doesn't matter what you call it for it has no matter at all. It's the invisibility between particles of matter, the confusion between states of understanding, the terrifying gap between one solemn belief and another.

Chaos can be found within each person as the great unconscious pit that follows consciousness all around. It's the emptiness that can appear at any moment, in any situation, without cause, and against all reason. Because of something said or simply left unsaid, a chasm can suddenly appear between people. A moment of silence can expand into an eternity. A little distancing or confusion can grow into an abyss that seems impossible to bridge. It happens all the time, within families, in marriages, between nations, even within the blessed orders of religion. Between one thing and another, the primal abyss is always a possibility. A little chaos goes a long way.

Cosmos and chaos are the two huge energies that make and unmake and remake everything. They are the all or nothing of this world; the grand Yea and the great Nay; all that can exist and nonexistence as well. The shape and motion of this world includes both cosmos and chaos, order and the lack of it in a constant and secret exchange under the skin of all of existence.

Some eras rise on the filling tides of cosmos as the breath of inspiration launches wondrous forms over the face of the earth. Temples arise that rival the mountains, sculptured deities speak from rock walls, complete musical forms appear in the dreams of people, and primordial ideas find conscious expression.

At other times, chaos tips the scales out of balance and throws everything into disarray. Empires rise but fall quickly, whole libraries become lost in the whirling sands, languages slip unspoken from the lips, and the breath of great ideas withdraws from the tongues of mankind.

Chaos threatens when it seems that people could end all of creation "with the push of a button;" as if a nihilistic aspect of mankind secretly aligns with the abyss, intrigued with the gaping maw at the edge of creation. Amidst overpopulation of the planet and greedy exploitation of the earth's resources, cosmos begins to slip towards chaos again.

To be modern is to be on the verge, at the edge and seemingly near the end. This period in which it seems that the final end could come from either natural disaster, a clash of cultures, or a showdown between deterministic religions can also be seen as a turn in the story of the cosmos, a return to the conditions of chaos that include both endings and beginnings, both the emptying of familiar forms and the renewing reservoir of cosmic life. For chaos was essential at the very beginning just as surely as it attends all the endings.

The cosmologies of the peoples of the earth tend to begin and end with chaos. The earth is the timebound middle ground where history suffers the endless exchange and mutual dance of chaos and cosmos. The world dips into the dark night of chaos at the end of each day and the dawn rescues the world from the endless sea of night each morning. Darkness and light, chaos and cosmos, lost and found; that's the world and we all live there.

Yet mythic images and ideas usually occur in groups of three. Two of anything tends towards simple opposition and static polarization. The third time is a charm and third things tend to add a new element to the opposing rhythm of back and forth. Myth favors third things and middle ways that go between the necessary tension made of any opposites. As above, so below with the middle caught between and ever on the verge of collapse or else being recreated again.

THE MESS IN THE MIDDLE

The cosmic middle ground used to be called the mesocosm, from the old Greek word *meso* or middle, as in "Mesolithic," and "Mesozoic." The mesocosm is the middle earth where the cosmic order and abysmal disorder as well as the bigger than big and smaller than small frequently meet and often collide. It's the world as we know it, the ground on which we walk with the gravities that keep us grounded and the tragedies that overwhelm us.

We dwell in the middle ground where the living green garment of nature and wondrous maze of culture meet and exchange, collide and divide. We are surrounded by it, born to it, immersed in it, dependent upon it, and in the long run, essential to it as well.

The mesocosm reflects and reacts to macrocosmic events such as sun spots and to microcosmic changes such as alterations in the micro-making of chlorophyll inside forests. It also suffers the distortions that result from dividing the nucleus to make weapons that threaten the balance of life on earth. In the living cosmology, humans act out the cosmic dance of creation and destruction, often without even knowing it.

Humanity stands and falls in the middle of the whole thing. Not because the earth sits at the mathematical center of the universe, but because the earth is the center of life for all earthly creatures. Like it or not, humans are cosmologically implicated, stuck in the thick of it, right in the messy middle where both chaos and cosmos can be felt and found.

When it seems that the whole thing might unravel or self-destruct it is the mesocosm rattling and shifting and being drawn into a cosmic turn with humans beings stumbling in the middle of the mess. For the mesocosm can get very messy before the hidden order of things can be found again.

Welcome to the chaos and the cosmos, welcome to the "chaosmos," as the poet said, but few were listening. Welcome to the "endarkenment" that follows the Enlightenment, to the dark times when the lights are on all the time, to the Kali Yuga and the Last Throw and the great throw-down. Welcome to the end of the world as they knew it and the loose ends of time's linear dispensation.

Welcome to the mess of the mesocosm, to the chaos of theories about what might happen next. Welcome to the remains of the day and the remainders of modernity, to the turning of the cosmos and the learning of the chaos. Welcome to the chaosmos where order and disorder dance, where ends and beginnings meet and miss and mess around with all the elements, as it was in the beginning and is again in the world always ending and without end amen, amen. For cosmos comes from chaos, order rises from the void and light must be born from the darkest hour of night's endless abyss.

In mythic tales chaos presents the original condition, the "prima materia," from which all matter and everything that comes to matter first arises. Chaos was there at the very beginning and it waits along all the edges and margins of life. Chaos is both the primal emptiness and the source of everything that comes into existence. Chaos is the pregnant disorder that both heralds The End and signals the beginning again.

Cosmos and chaos play a continuous game of hide-and-seek with only a thin veil of illusion between them. Chaos is the empty-fullness that secretes the full-emptiness back into play. Cosmos depends on Chaos, everything does—even us. The return of cosmic order and cosmic sense always happens at the edge of the abyss, on the brink of disaster where life and beauty and meaning are snatched from the teeth of chaos. At the bottom of the bottomless chasm the world returns again.

Any real change includes a period of chaos, often a brush with death. Each step into the abyss has an initiatory potential. Each step taken into the territory betwixt and between one thing and another, between one stage of life and the next, betwixt one epoch and what follows has the potential to change and renew life. In order to make a real change a person or a culture must consciously step beyond their usual condition and enter unknown territories before life can find a true path onward again.

As things unravel in the middle and the end seems near, the two ways to turn for solace and direction are deep within and out at the edge where the imagination of the cosmos continues as a grand, never-ending story. Whatever the lunacy on earth, the moon continues on with its hide-and-seek ways. The Milky Way whirls through the dark reaches of cosmic night. The macrocosmic world continues its infinite song whether those on earth are tuned in or zoning out.

BEING AN OLD SOUL

The microcosmic world also continues, as matter and energy exchange places and the infinite, cellular dance of life proceeds in unseen ways. And inside each human life the dance also continues. The human soul has a mythic propensity and cosmological instinct for making something out of nothing. The soul can hold views as opposite as order and disorder, as contrary as hate and love, as exclusive as progress and collapse. It registers how often things fall apart and finds endless ways to hold body and spirit together. The soul comes from the chaosmos, it knows that chaos and cosmos are in cahoots.

The soul survives all the false hopes and lost dreams and sudden reversals that the presence of chaos requires. Unlike the rational mind, the soul prefers to wander and deviate; it lingers and languishes and draws secret nourishment from defeat and dissipation as well as from order and success. It follows unseen patterns that include both loss and renewal, both catastrophic collapse and the little redemptions that make life possible on earth.

At times a "double-minded" awareness is required; not a split condition or a dissociated state, but a capacity for handling dualities, a facility for opposing arguments, a comfort within conflicts, a preference for paradox, an instinct for living in the ironies and adjusting to the twists of fate. Losing the sense of paradox means missing the point of what the tensions in the world are pointing at. The old soul has affinities for chaos even while it dreams of cosmos again.

Chaos also includes the warp in things, the weird way each existing thing is cast upon the loom of the world. Each soul carries its "twist of fate," the fatality woven within it to begin with, as well as, the hidden uniqueness that makes life worth living all the way out, no matter how desperate and despairing things might become.

The old soul that dwells at the core of each person has a tolerance for chaos and an instinct for survival. Not the simple biology of the survival of the fittest, but a complex involvement with hidden aspects of creation that only become known when the chips are down and there's nothing else to do but take on a bigger imagination of the cosmos and find one's place within it.

Most apocalyptic stories include visions of a regenerated world. In the end, the issue is not complete annihilation but surviving until the cosmic turning turns things all around. A willingness to face The End is often required for new ideas of survival to be discovered. The sense of the end-times and last days must be entered in order to find the creative imagination that can reveal paths of survival and threads of renewal as chaos winds its wicked way back to cosmos again.

The soul naturally sees with a darkened eye. It relates to the dusty light of both dusk and dawn. It seeks the kind of knowledge that knows its own shadow. At certain times in the course of life it becomes necessary to become an old soul, to wander amongst the paradoxes and feel the way along by an inner Braille and a willingness to stumble and fall into the truth of things.

Each initiatory passage requires that we become lost to all that we know. The keys that unlock the doors of wisdom have to be found in the darkness or else fashioned from some loss. If the keys were in the light everyone would already have found them.

Remember the old Mullah who lost the only key to his little house? A friend found him on hands and knees in the middle of the night. There he was down on all fours in the bare circle of the light that fell from the globe of a single lamp post. It was apparent that he was searching for something and examining every inch of the ground before him.

The friend bent down as well and asked if something was lost. The Mullah explained that he had lost the key to the door of his house and was locked out in the dark in the middle of the night. The friend willingly knelt on the ground and joined the search. What are friends for if not to help when we get lost in the darkness and can't find our way home?

After a long time of silent searching with no discoveries, the friend asked the Mullah: "Are you sure you dropped it right here in the light below this lamp post?" "No," answered the Mullah, "I'm quite sure I dropped it over there." He stood up and pointed some distance away where darkness seemed to extend endlessly beyond the little arc of light.

"If the missing key that alone can unlock the door was lost over in there in the darkness, why on earth are we searching here?" asked the friend. "Because this is where the light is," declared the Mullah.

So it usually goes. People follow the lead of the old Mullah who preferred looking for the missing key in the light cast by the little self that remains afraid of the darkness and the unknown nearby. Parts of us prefer manufactured light with its predictable circle of limited radiance. We stay amid the relative successes of projects generated by the little self and become reconciled to remaining outside the dwelling of our own soul.

We study the terrain others have cast some light upon, yet cannot find the key that unlocks our own inner presence. The circle of light provided by social concerns seems so much more inviting and promising than the huge darkness just beyond our knowing. Yet at certain points in life, the issue is no longer entering the little door of the self, nor even surviving another night.

On certain occasions, the issue becomes the willingness to enter the darkness in order to find a key that belongs strangely to us and can open the inner door. Those who try to avoid the inner darkness also miss the inner light. Those who avoid chaos at any cost wind up subject to it. Each return to the doors of eternity involves the remembrance of the pain of existing. Uncertainty, pain, and fear precede the locating of the key to the inner life, the way labor pains and worries are required to initiate birth.

No one can find that for us, not even a friend of the soul. Yet, it is there exactly where most choose not to look. A friend helps by asking whether we are looking in the right place or not. Friends, stories, and dreams are there to warn us of the common delusions. Especially now, in the afterglow of the Enlightenment, with lights on twenty-four hours a day and people claiming to offer the keys to success and the secrets of life for a certain fee or else an agreement to follow dogmatic rules.

Becoming an old soul and having an inner sense for finding places of refuge and ways to practice awareness doesn't require reaching a certain age as much as growing ancient now and becoming wise enough to know where to look for the key that opens the inner doors. The soul sense is part of the lost-and-found of this life where becoming lost is a requirement for anything that would be found. Darkness is required for the light to appear. On certain occasions we have to bend low, enter the darkness and see with a darkened eye if we would recover the key that unlocks the mystery of the soul.

IV

The Great Way

CHAPTER 12

BACK FROM THE ASHES

Cosmology may be the oldest art as each tribal group, no matter how small in numbers, no matter how simple in technology, must explain the entire world. From the beginning people have had to deal with the huge forces of darkness and light, eternity and time that throw this world back and forth between two opposite poles of creation and destruction.

Water and fire are also opposites that need to be kept in balance for the earth to sustain life. An eternal fire burns at the center of the earth and requires that water be spread all over its surface. There are tons of flammable gases underneath the great ice caps. It takes a great amount of water in its various states to balance the intensity of fire on earth. The earth is in the middle of a balancing act between fire and water. Too much water and the earth drowns in a flood; too much fire and the earth is consumed in flames.

Water is ubiquitous. It turns up and flows down and runs through everywhere. Fire tends to hide inside things and erupts under specific conditions. Once ignited, fire can go from warming to burning quickly and it can use almost anything for fuel. Fire is a problem that way, it can warm and illuminate, but can also become a rage that consumes all that exists.

Once upon a time, the elemental of fire got out of hand. Instead of simply warming the world fire came to dominate the other elements.

Soon everything became overheated and a conflagration began to spread throughout the world, eventually consuming every living thing. For whatever reasons, fire went out of control. The world burned up and all that remained of the verdant earth was a mass of ashes. The fire reduced the singing green forests to cinders and ash, even the mountains were melted down. Nothing remained standing or moving on the earth.

It happened that two beings, Icanchu and Chuna, had been visiting in the otherworld when the great conflagration occurred. When they returned to the common world all they could see was an endless sea of ash. They desired to return to their original homeland, but everywhere they looked, looked the same. They couldn't tell what was what, where they were at, or where to go.

Suddenly the trickster appeared and advised them to find their place of origin by pointing their index fingers straight ahead. When their fingers began to turn down of their own accord they would be pointing to the place of their origins.

Icanchu and Chuna happened to be bird-beings, so the business of fingers and wings was complicated. It's difficult to picture this process of pointing and flying, of having bird wings and human fingers. Suffice it to say that it was a long time ago during a period when people could be like birds and birds could be like humans. Icanchu and Chuna were a pair of bird-beings, birds on one hand and human beings on the other.

They had been in the otherworld, yet they had origins on the earth as well. The old people believed that all humans were naturally that way, able to live in two worlds, maybe required to do so. Sometimes they were simply people, sometimes closer to animal spirits. That was back in the time when animals were revered and to be "like an animal" indicated having additional powers, such as sensing danger or a storm coming, or the ability to fly over the earth, to rise above problems and see them more clearly.

Having been in the otherworld during the great burnout, Icanchu and Chuna now flew over the devastation and somehow managed to extend their index fingers before them. They trusted the knowledge given to them by the trickster, for they knew that tricksters have to do with the tricks of creation as well as with destruction. They knew that the whole world was full of tricks and hidden energies; perhaps there another trick remained in creation that could start things going again.

As they traveled over the endless wasteland of ashes their index fingers began to bend towards the earth and soon were pointing firmly downwards. The two travelers followed their fingers down; they descended right into the ash. They felt that they might be back home, yet only ashes remained of all that they had known before. They were in the aftermath of everything, stuck in the ashes of existence.

As soon as they touched the earth, the two remaining beings realized they felt quite hungry. They began to dig in the ashes in case something might remain that could serve as food. Icanchu unearthed a chunk of charcoal. While looking at it he felt a deep longing for trees. Once upon a time the place of their origins had been like a garden resplendent with greenery and many species of trees. He considered that the piece of charcoal had to be the remainder of one of those trees that made their home a beautiful place.

Suddenly the thought struck him that drums were also remainders of trees. The people used to make drums from certain trees and use them for dances and for ceremonies. First a tree would appear in someone's dream; that gave the permission for cutting it down and making drums from it. Without thinking further, Icanchu began to play that burnt-out, leftover piece of wood as if it were a drum.

Soon enough Icanchu became infected by his own rhythm and began to dance. As long as he was dancing he might as well sing. In the midst of the ashes of creation Icanchu sang and danced and played upon his charcoal drum. There was nothing to eat, nothing but ash to look at and nothing else to do; besides, dancing and playing gave him some courage. He danced and played all day long while Chuna observed and seemed to meditate on the proceedings. At the end of the day Icanchu became tired. He lay down and fell into a deep sleep right there in the ashes of the place of origins, in the ashes of the end of the day.

When dawn came and chased the darkness from the world, Icanchu went to look at the piece of charcoal that had been the drum of the day before. He could see a tender green shoot coming out of the blackened husk of charcoal. Icanchu began to sing again; he danced around that shoot and sang and sang. The tendril seemed to grow from being bathed in the song. It grew larger and longer. Soon enough, that little tendril had grown to be like a branch and the pair of seekers took some refuge from the burning sun in its tender shade.

Icanchu kept singing and dancing and as the day drew on the tendril of life grew steadily and began to look like a slender tree trunk. In no time at all, the trunk thickened and put forth long green branches that reached out in all four directions. There it stood in the middle of the expanse of ashes, the only vertical expression, the only green intention, the only tree on the earth.

People say that it was the Firstborn Tree, the Ancestor Tree that grew again from the ashes of the earth, from the charcoal remainder, and from the song and drumming of Icanchu. They say it was the original "helper tree" come back from the ashes of the end, able to rise from the devastation and conflagration that had consumed the world.

Some say it was the same tree that shamans and healers went to whenever they sought knowledge of what caused a certain illness and what might serve to cure it. The relationship between trees and people is an ancient one. It would make some sense that things could start up again when that ancient and mysterious relationship became renewed and revitalized.

Icanchu danced around the tree that had grown from the little tendril that had sprouted from the charcoal, that had lain in the ashes of the fire, that had consumed most of the world. While dancing away, Icanchu's foot struck a stone buried loosely in the sea of ashes that had once been the earth. He picked up the stone and threw it right at the amazing tree. It's hard to explain this sudden action and change of attitude. When the dancer found another stone, he threw that at the tree as well.

After singing to the tree and dancing around it and even taking shelter under its spreading branches, Icanchu began to chuck rocks at it from all directions. You might call it instinct, or foolishness or another of those mistakes that happen in the vicinity of important trees. Perhaps the instinct for destruction travels with the creative instinct and they have to return to the world together. Creation and destruction are twin forces like beginning and ending. In a given situation it can be difficult to know which moves the story of life along.

Then again, it may have been a touch of that trickster energy that hangs around whenever creation or destruction happens to enter a situation. At any rate, Icanchu kept firing rocks at the firstborn tree. He tossed the stones with the same enthusiasm and abandon that he had devoted to dancing and singing to the tendril that sprouted from the darkness of the charcoal. Throughout all of this, Chuna sat in silence, observing everything.

Each time Icanchu threw a stone it would hit a branch and each time a branch would break off from the tree, it would fall to the ash-covered earth. The strange thing was that each broken branch immediately took root in the ashes. The branches of the firstborn tree took root wherever they fell and soon multiplied so that each branch became a tree and each tree soon became a growing forest. Not only that, but each branch gave rise to a different species of tree. Once all the limbs had fallen, there were countless species of trees and full-blown forests greenly growing and wildly lifting their branches up and sending roots deep into the old earth.

Where the charcoal had been set, where the tendril had appeared, there now stood the source tree, the Medicine Tree that had been described in old stories. The little tendril born of darkness and drumming, of singing and dancing turned out to be the tree of many names. Some called it the Tree of Origins, others the Spirit Tree, or the Shaman's Tree, the Test Tree, the Tree of the Knowledge of Good and Evil, the Tree of Remembering and

Forgetting, the Tree of Enlightenment, the Tree of Life.

It was also the Tree of Renewal that completes the pattern that permeates all trees: life, death, and renewal. Icanchu sang it back to life. He pounded it like a drum. He danced around it and even threw rocks at it. All those things contributed to the growing up and branching out of the tree behind the trees. After the branches fell to the ground and all the species of the forests grew back, the animals began to appear again and eventually more people appeared as well.

Each year after that, when the fruit trees began to grow heavy with ripening fruit, the people would gather for a ceremony. Amidst the fruit-laden branches people would dance and sing and play on drums made from certain trees. They would throw little stones at the trees and knock down some ripened fruit. They would act out the dance of creation and destruction and sing the songs of ripening and renewal.

They imitated the actions of Icanchu and they would sit quietly and contemplate this world that grows back from its own ashes, just like Chuna observing all the antics that constitute the back and forth of destruction and creation. The people understood that the dancing, singing, and playing, even the contrary action of throwing rocks, helped to regenerate the life tree that exists at the center, in the place of origins.

ASHES TIME

A towering tree can be reduced to a pile of ash; everything can wind up in the ashes. Ashes appear in fairy tales where the youngest sister has been denied her true position and forced to labor in obscurity amidst the cinders. Ashes begin the period of Lent and the annual ceremonies reminding how Christ descended to the underworld before rising again. Ancient and contemporary "sadhus" who give up common social roles and seek awakenings through ascetic practices cover themselves in ashes to indicate that they have died to the daily world with all its material concerns. And times of ashes also occur inside the lives of people when tragedies strike, when illness enters, when sorrow and grief change the landscape and leave dust in the mouth.

As both natural disasters and manmade tragedies occur with increasing frequency and deepening intensities, this era between one thing and another can be seen as a time of ashes. The danger now exists that nuclear proliferation combined with terrorism or simple foolishness might spark a conflagration that consumes the earth. At the same time, global warming threatens to melt the protective ice caps and release highly flammable gases that could set even the oceans on fire.

Symbolically, we're in the ashes, in one of those periods when it seems that all the great hopes and grand dreams for life might simply turn to ash. Some people argue over the presence and importance of severe climate change. Some simply deny the whole thing. Yet young people have to grow into the troubles as well as grow up to the potentials of the times to which they are born. Youth awaken to life in the midst of life. They enter life in the way that Icanchu and Chuna suddenly appear with a longing for home and with a view of the devastation of life and the ashes all around.

The young take in the world like birds taking partly digested food from their parents. In order to survive they must digest things that the older folks have only partly chewed over. If notions of a great disaster are in the air, they breathe that in. Older folks may turn away from certain threats in hopes that they will depart the earth before the ashes accumulate. Young people have to face into the storms and disasters of life and must find ways to see their way through.

A story like that of Icanchu and the charcoal drum looks directly at the possibility of the earth becoming overheated and overwhelmed by fire. It contemplates a time of ashes and considers what the human spirit might do should all the wonders of life become reduced to residues and remainders. Since the tale arises from a mythical and cosmological tradition, it views disaster, even worldwide conflagration from another perspective that begins with a vantage point in the otherworld.

Icanchu and his companion Chuna happen to be elsewhere when the all-consuming fire becomes unleashed upon the earth. There's a suggestion that being in touch with the otherworld might protect people from harms that happen in this realm. Not a "rapture" that allows certain elect souls to escape the storms and droughts and inflammations of this world; but a way to view the problems from the ground of myth and imagination.

The companions who alone survive the incineration of life on earth enter from the unseen realm, from the world behind this world, as a result they don't succumb to the time of ashes. Instead of being consumed by the flames of conflict and the apocalyptic fires of fear and terror, they remain connected to the song of creation and the rhythms of eternity that can regenerate life from the ashes of the world as we know it.

Many creation stories begin with a word or a sound, an initial vibration that continues to reverberate and echo through the world. The tale of Icanchu, Chuna, and the charcoal drum uses sound and rhythm to regenerate life after a time of consumption and destruction. It depicts a reversal of those creation tales where the creator gods breathe life into humanity and start the language of life and the cycles and rhythms of the incarnated world. This re-creation tale begins in a time of ashes, in the aftermath of creation; it requires that beings living in this realm kick-start creation again.

Like young folks who have to see the whole thing as possible and full of hidden potentials regardless of the evidence of loss and decline, Icanchu and Chuna represent enduring inner qualities of the soul. Icanchu acts the role of the eternal youth, the "puer aeternus" that ever leaps and flies and dances in the recesses of the human soul. Chuna presents the contrasting presence of the eternal and constant companion, the inner reflective aspect that travels with the soul throughout the course of life.

Icanchu responds to the devastation and meets the desiccating winds of destruction with his own ways of dancing and singing. His unfettered imagination sees an instrument in the puny and charred remains of a forest of living trees. Faced with the ashes of all that went before he remembers that drums come from trees and that's enough to set him dancing and singing, despite and possibly because of the dust heap of existence all around.

The idea here is not that of allowing the world to self-destruct and then try dancing upon the corpse. Rather, it involves sustaining the vitality of nature and renewing the beauty of human culture by entering the dance of life despite the presence of disasters and threats of extinction. Any who would truly dance must give themselves up to the dance. A real dance makes a person wholehearted and causes the dancer to become at least momentarily whole. Wholeness speaks to wholeness as the dance provokes life hidden in the darkness. Finding moments of wholeness helps to regenerate life from the source of life.

By treating the burned-out remnant of a tree as a resonant instrument, by dancing and singing with it, the basic vitality of life is invited to return to the world. Didn't traditional funerals end with music and dance? Only modern people keep such an extreme distance from the corpse and remain solemn in the face of death. A whole funeral honors the life of the deceased, pays respect to their passing, and acknowledges that death waits for all who enter the roads of life. And a whole funeral separates the dead from the living.

Death and the losses it occasions must be given their due. Yet respect means to look again and a thorough view of the funeral grounds includes both the presence of life and the absence caused by death. Funerals used to give death and disintegration their due before turning back to the rhythms of life. After the wake and the open grieving people would reawaken to the rhythms of life. In the reversal that concludes the funeral march those who remain alive re-enter the common world, often while singing and playing music.

Remember the "second line"? The funeral band plays dirges and laments; it sets the tone, opens the paths of grief and leads the way to the burial grounds. After the corpse or the ashes have been placed in the ground everyone must turn around. Now, the band walks at the rear to keep a separation between the living and the dead. The bereaved family may wear some ashes; people used to do that, for the death fell on them as well. Yet, life must be remembered even in the proximity of death.

Music can be fashioned for the road to the grave and for the way back to life. The emotions inside everyone know both directions. To be truly alive means to go back and forth on the roads of life and death.

Icanchu was that kind of musician. He saw instruments where others see only loss and darkness and decimation. He allowed the rhythm of life to flow in his veins even when the big funeral had come around. He accepted the time of ashes, but also accepted whatever inspiration he found within those times. By connecting the charcoal to its roots in the Tree of Life he instigated a renewal of life from within the darkness. Life often waits to be found where most see only loss and lifelessness. In both creation and re-creation tales life comes from what seems to be lifeless.

Icanchu and Chuna bring a perspective from the otherworld, the world behind this world, the one that imbued this realm with life to begin with and that can do so again. Icanchu acts with unhindered instincts for survival and with full imagination for what gives life its music and meaningful rhythms. When people feel lost in life they have lost their rhythm for life. In the midst of the ashes of life it's necessary to find one's internal rhythm again.

Not only that, Icanchu attacks the source of life as well as incants songs to it. Once the delicate thread of existence has been coaxed from the dark husk of lifelessness, the singer turns to stone thrower. He who just sang the song of life to the tender tendrils of existence turns to throwing rocks and knocking branches off the Tree of Life. This can cause a deep shock to those who develop a false reverence for life and try to solve the dilemmas of existence by following some predetermined set of rules.

Life breaks all the rules all the time in its pursuit of diversity and multiplicity. There are times when reverence and respect, when care and consideration are required to protect and strengthen the threads of life. And there are times when people must take the hard issues in hand and act with some abandon or else life can drain from the branches of existence.

In the time of ashes both the protective feelings for life and the instinctive expressions of it become required.

ENTER THE TRICKSTER

Wasn't it the trickster who told the two survivors how to find the origins of their lives again? Staying alive and helping the great diversity that makes up the realms of both nature and culture requires some knowledge of the tricks of existence. Many creation stories involve tricksters right at the start. Some tales begin with a god who shapes a perfect world, yet something seems off. There's not enough laughter in it, or mistakes are treated as sins, or there's not enough diversity in the way people make love.

Then the trickster comes along in the form of raven, a coyote, or a snake and people begin to do things backwards or see things the other way around. Icanchu finds a stone and has the urge to throw it. A strange bone in him aims at the Tree of Life and lets it go. Bam, a whole branch becomes dislodged from the medicine tree; yet instead of starting a new disaster, the contrary gesture generates more life. This surprising energy inherent in life continues to confound those who try to control things too much or insist on false reverence when life calls for wholehearted and even reckless involvement.

Tricksters play essential roles in folk myths throughout the world. They throw dirt as well as toss rocks; they play with feces and throw it at people, even at god. They keep the dirt and the earth and the earthiness in the stories of life. They appear especially when the old order of the world needs to change; they are change agents and provocateurs and wise in wise-guy ways. They bring strange and unexpected pieces of wisdom that help to kick-start creation when it has collapsed or simply lapsed.

Icanchu accepts the instinct to throw stones just as he accepted the intuition to play the charcoal as a drum. He's consistent in his primordial responses to the world around him. He acts both as artist and as trickster; how else could it be? In the proximity of the Tree of Life all the opposites meet and become life-generating. The presence of the origin tree makes originality possible; when near it life can go *contra naturum*, against one's apparent nature, even against the typical ways of nature. It is the nature of Nature to change and to respond to changes.

Those who make environmental concerns into a new form of Puritanism remain distant from what truly preserves and regenerates life. Life on earth is not tame; rather, it involves a dance that invites all the senses and the entire range of emotions and soulful emanations. Sometimes a little anger thrown at the branches of existence or at the false solemnities of social institutions creates just enough conflict to inspire more diversity of life forms.

In this old myth the stone element becomes the change agent necessary for regenerating the diversity of the living world. The stone element enters through a disruption. Stones are dense and hard and it's hard to resist throwing them when near the water and sometimes when near the trees. Yet stones have qualities within themselves. Stones, like bones and shells, are the slow stories of this earth. They are the memory elements that can reveal the history of the other elements on earth.

In order for life to thrive and diversify, many shapes and forms, many feelings, unusual attitudes and spontaneous gestures must enter the equation. The re-creation of the world had to be just as inclusive as the original creation. In a sense, the two companions landed, not simply at the place of their origins, but at the very center of life where all the elements convene, where everything makes more sense—even nonsense.

In seeking to find home the companions find the center where all the elements meet and the Tree of Life regenerates. The element of earth remained underneath the ash, partly as the anchor for the tree of renewal and partly as the home place, the place of origin for all the children of the earth. The real home for earthlings turns out to be the center of everything; and the center also turns out to be the beginning, the place where life began and can begin again. The center becomes revealed as the place of renewal; finding the tree at the center also means finding ways to begin it all again.

Everyone searches for home and home turns out to be the center of our lives. The real home is the center within each life and each return to that inner center not only calms and heals the person and makes the person whole, but also adds some healing and wholeness to the world around us. When the end seems near it's time to seek the center within and find ways to be central to the healing of the scorched and scarred earth around us. The great tragedies and dramas of life and the threat of it all ending try to return humanity to an awareness of the eternal presence of the divine waiting at the center of each life and all of life.

THE TREE AT THE CENTER

The strange little re-creation tale leads from the ashen remains of both nature and civilization to the tree hidden at the center of all life. The unifying tree has roots that plunge deep into the underworld and branches that reach up to the heavens. The original symbolism of the Tree of Life involved a mythical sense of a world axis, the "axis mundi" around which creation was created, the unified center where all dualities and oppositions come together.

The Tree of Life appears in many forms and can be found wherever and whenever people manage to find the center of life again. As center point the tree remains eternally still; yet as the living, breathing Tree of Life it presents a core image of constant change. It grows repeatedly from the same unseen roots. It is rooted in the imagination, in the living Soul of the World and the old soul of humankind where it must be nourished by dreams and longings, by songs and dances that make things whole if only for a moment. Each return to the tree at the center becomes a return to the origins of life and thus a renewal of the world.

The Tree of Life is the Paradise Tree and the Tree of Imagination; it is the Tree of Fertility and the family tree; the Tree of Ascent and Descent where the shamans seek the heights of spirit and the depths of soul; it's the Tree of Sacrifice, the Tree of Death; it's the "hanging tree" and the Tree of Enlightenment. Call it the Tree of Life and Death, the Tree of the Sun Dance, the Shaman Tree and the Tree of the Cross on which Christ hangs. It's the Otherworld Tree, the Tree Behind the Tree; it is the Bodhi Tree of stillness where Buddha broke through the spell of the world and found enlightenment; it is the cosmic pillar that the shaman climbs in ecstatic trance.

It's the glowing Christmas tree in the midst of winter darkness and the cross on which the savior hangs; it's the hollow center of the Navaho Reed of Life and the mast to which Ulysses remains bound; it's the Tree of the Ancestors, the White Tree of Peace, and the Tree of the Knowledge of Good and Evil that can divide things, open the oppositions, and set them in conflict all over again.

The Tree of Life has always been there; it stands in the midst of the archetypal pack of eternal symbols that keep arising into human awareness. In one sense it is less real than any tree in a nearby garden or forest. In another sense, both a deeper and higher sense, the symbolic tree is more real than real. In that mythic sense it is the original tree and the mother of all trees, the essence and source and sense of being that gives vertical shape and green life to all trees. Seen in that essential way, any tree can become the Tree of Life and awaken the deep memories rooted in the soul.

Symbols are needed to bring the mind and the heart to the doors of truth. Truth appears differently to different people and a genuine symbol appears differently to each viewer. Say Tree of Life and all people see a tree of some kind within themselves. A genuine symbol reflects back to seers and seekers, the truth they already carry inside. A symbol helps reveal what the seekers otherwise conceal from themselves.

In the old roots of language, tree and truth are related, parts of the same branching family of words. Relatives of truth include truce and troth, trust and betrothal; and tryst as well. So, people carve hearts in trees and "plight their troth," marrying themselves to a truth of longing before actually "tying the knot." People "knock on wood" in hopes that what they say is true or might become so. Making a truce often involves an olive branch, a sign of trust ever since Athena, the goddess of wisdom, planted a sprig of it at the center of the great city of Athens that still bears her name.

Truth is a living thing that must be fashioned again and again from the roots of learning and branches of experience. Each soul, each era, each culture must cultivate its own sense of life and its own symbols of truth. Yet the living tree at the center remains the symbolic axis that penetrates and connects all the branching thoughts and images that constitute the religions and philosophies of humankind.

All the branches of truth and meaning secretly grow from the same unseen roots. All spiritual paths secretly lead to the center and to the ever-branching Tree of Life, but only when they are followed far enough. The tree at the beginning is also the tree at the center and the cross at the end as well. Major symbols serve to hold beginning, middle, and end together. When The End seems near, the beginning is also close and the center is trying to surface again.

Icanchu and Chuna are symbols of the relationship between the human actor and his divine twin who ever observes the dramas and reversals of fortune while remaining faithful to the dream and the dance intended in that life. The divine twin of the soul watches and witnesses the entire adventure as each soul tries to return to the tree at the center of its inner garden.

The story of Icanchu's Drum depicts the renewal of the earth from the ashes and it includes the rebirth of a living symbol. From the ashes of all that went before comes a symbol that in turn brings the world back from the brink of annihilation. When life on earth seems threatened and the usual centers cannot hold, it's time to take up the imagination and rhythms of real presence and become a branch of the kind of knowing that recalls the subtle ground of unity and draws upon the roots of the divine hidden amongst the ashes of the world.

CHAPTER 13

THE TREE BEHIND THE TREE

Each soul harbors a sense of divine meaning within and expects a call that awakens it to a life aligned with an inner sense of purpose. No one can prove this with logical arguments, just the way no one can easily know the souls of others or measure the size of their hearts. This involves reasons beyond reason and meanings that precede common learning. This involves the origins of the soul and agreements made before it entered this realm of time and place.

A story still told in West Africa describes how each human soul enters the world. Before birth, souls reside in a subtle realm somewhere beyond this world of ashes, sticks and stones. They remain in that ancestral zone able to observe life on earth until they become intrigued with something they perceive. Some image moves the soul and that motion carries it towards incarnation.

The image that moves a soul to enter life remains central to it throughout its time on earth. During the course of life the core imagination continually tries to surface through dreams and dramas, through mistakes and failings, through the lovings and losings that occur to each soul on earth.

As soon as the soul begins to move towards the door of birth, it encounters a divine being. This representative of the eternal realm gives the soul an outline of the gifts and talents it will bring to life as well as a sense of its purpose in going there. This is the meeting of soul and spirit that precedes each life. This first friend of life describes what will be inscribed in the soul, the inner sense of what that life must be about. This encounter represents the first lesson the soul learns from its first teacher and inner companion, for the "divine twin" remains with the individual soul.

Each soul has a divine agreement, an agreed-upon sense of purpose and direction in life, an "imaginal" reason for being born and a destiny to seek and learn in living form. Only after entering such a divine agreement can the soul continue on the path to its appointment with birth. The inner companion and guide tends to the core of the soul, keeping it connected to the original imagination that harbors both the limits known as fate and the longings that intuit destiny.

After the first meeting of the soul and the divine twin the two companions continue on the road to earthly life when suddenly, the soul sees an extraordinary tree before it. The beauty of the tree moves the soul; it feels akin to that rooted presence and can't help but embrace it. On the way to life on earth the soul embraces the Tree of Life that stands where the roots of eternity connect to the branching moments of time. At this point the tree of many shapes appears as the Tree of Forgetfulness, as soon as the soul embraces the tree it forgets the agreement just made with the divine twin. And then it is born.

The soul can't help it, it must touch and embrace the tree that stands so close to the doors of life. Yet, after making a deal with the divine it completely forgets the details of that agreement. The moment of birth involves a forgetting, so that each birth is a partial birth and the soul will try to be born again and again at each opening and turning along the road of life. The divine companion remains nearby and tries in subtle ways to remind us of what we had to forget in order to enter this world where forgetting seems to be increasing all the time.

It's no accident that a tree stands amidst this old teaching tale that helps us to remember that unique qualities and hidden purpose are seeded in the soul from the beginning. We are indelibly and undeniably connected to trees. We need the oxygen they offer us and need them to transform the carbon dioxide we cannot help but exude whether we be arguing or meditating quietly. We began essential exchanges with trees before birth and continued them with the first breath we took in this world.

The connection between the trees in this world and the tree behind the tree from which they come remains a symbolic thread that ties the eternal realm to the time-bound world. Yet the unifying Tree of Life has been mostly forgotten during the battles over ownership of various lands and supposedly sacred grounds. Some forgetting also occurs before people undertake the massive destruction of trees and primal forests, some disconnection must precede such blindness. Along with the loss of unifying symbols and sacred connections to the earth, the distinct knowledge that each soul carries gifts and purposes has been forgotten as well.

The human soul begins its unique and surprising journey after embracing the Tree of Forgetfulness and does not complete the real course of life until it finds some form of the Tree of Life again. Each person is both a knower and a lost soul; each innately inclined in certain ways, yet needing to awaken to the sense of meaning and direction carried within. Each seeks for the awakening presence of the tree that is breathing, in the garden of the soul, in the inner bowers of human imagination.

Remember the story of the Buddha: he awakened while meditating at the base of the Tree of Enlightenment. The presence of the tree was no accident there either, something of the living tree often appears in stories of seeking and finding. The Bodhi Tree protected him as he struggled with the demons of distraction and forgetting; but a tree grew inside him as well. In order to become the Buddha he had to find the way his soul intended to grow within and branch out from there. Later, his teaching would take root in many lands, taking on a different shape in each place.

Something important had been lost at that time and the elegance and rootedness of the great tree helped the seeker to find it within. The tree offered its essential way of being; how to sit in the world, how to settle upon inner roots and breathe and branch and protect life while producing eternal fruits. Whenever the inner life awakens, the Tree of Remembrance branches again nearby, for the garden at the center and the seeds of life and destiny are also close.

All genuine learning involves a radical remembering of who we already are and what our soul intends to bring to life through us. Usually, it takes a distinct crisis to bring the soul to the edge of awareness where the "original agreement" with the divine twin comes back to mind. Sometimes the twin appears as a dream or a guide in a dream, for the soul ever dreams of its own inner shape and purpose in being.

Sometimes the twin appears as an act of conscience. Remember old Socrates: he had a singular conscience with a limited vocabulary. Whenever the old philosopher was about to take a wrong turn in the crossroads of life the soul companion or inner daimon would simply and emphatically say: No. A bit of a negative style with that divine twin; yet some are innately inclined to go the way of the *via negativa*. For others, the inner daimon seems to say yes to everything and they travel a road of repeated acceptance.

Sometimes the twin appears in the eyes and heart of another who reflects back to us an immediate and knowing sense of love. For the other sees who we are in essence and how we are aimed in this life. Those Friends of the Self become teachers and lovers of the dream within us. They perceive and reflect the soul companion that also looks out from our eyes. That kind of gazing usually starts some kind of dancing or a fierce study that opens the gates of the gardens of knowledge.

Yea or nay, sitting or dancing, the soul tries to awaken fully to the dream and imagination that moved it to this world to begin with. Even if the purpose of a particular soul is to point away from the things of this world, the inner fruits must grow here before the movement away becomes ripe and sweet. All the genuine arts and true practices offer ways of moving around the Tree of Life and ripening the inner fruits of presence. Anything that moves those fruits from sour to sweet is a practice; anything that adds to the beauty of the garden of life is an art.

RIPE AND UNRIPE

Any genuine attention to the soul garden acts like an inner sun warming our lives and helping to ripen the inner fruits. The inner tree grows as we live, where we live; trying to express why we live. Twisted by storms of confusion, weathered by internal climates, withered in some places, and bearing strange fruit in others, at the end we stand like an old tree leaning at life.

Each soul harbors a garden where a true story dwells in seed form and waits to be watered with attention and nourished with genuine emotion. The roots of the soul are eternal, yet the branches reach into time and would bear fruit amongst the living. If a person has found a path of meaning in the world, the inner fruits ripen and become a resource and nourishment inside as well as a source of sweetness and reassurance to those we encounter on the way.

If the fruits of the soul fail to ripen they bear a bitter legacy that leaks into life. This inner bitterness tarnishes the subtle beauty of the world and eats away at the roots of meaning. Bitterness and wisdom cannot dwell in the same place. Unless something ripens within and becomes as a fruit ready to be shared and enjoyed a person grows bitter with age. Bitter or sweet, the soul tends to grow one way or the other.

Before any true awakening or genuine maturing of the hidden unity, the opposites within must intensify. For the opposites meet wherever the Tree of Life appears, be it in the inner garden or the outer world. The tree of forgetting precedes the tree of remembrance and the Tree of the Knowledge of Good and Evil must be encountered if the Tree of Eternal Life would be found again.

People argue about the source and meaning of evil acts found in all parts of this world where light and dark mix as often as day and night exchange places. An old meaning of *evil* was simply "unripe." Until the soul begins to grow towards its own sense of fullness and awareness it remains unripe, "green" in the wrong way. If the inner motion of the soul be strongly denied the fruits become bitter and vile as the rejected inner seeds spread conflict and division.

No amount of good intentions or positive ideas can remove evil from this world; only that more people learn to ripen the seeds they carry within and find ways to assist meaningful and purposeful things to blossom and ripen in the garden of reality. When something in this world becomes ripe and ready it becomes "good;" "good enough to eat," and beautiful to behold. Until then it remains like unripened fruit, more likely to produce sour grapes and bitter feelings.

BEYOND GOOD AND EVIL

The Tree of the Knowledge of Good and Evil marks a place where the tension of the opposites must be entered and learned from. It was once called the Tree of Division, for the knowledge it offers involves the polarities that permeate life on earth. Good and evil, life and death, inner and outer, self and other, truth and falsehood, left and right goes the road where everything is polarized before anything can ripen.

Maturing the fruits of knowledge requires bearing the tension of the opposites that inhabit the inner life and the outer world. Any unity follows a season of tension and being caught in thorny issues. Choosing one side of a dilemma too quickly means being one-sided and blind in one eye. Better to suffer some darkness while things ripen within than to grab the nearest idea or system of belief and claim that as the only way to grow or to avoid evil.

Those who insist on dividing everything into good and evil overlook the genuine nature of this complex world. For, opposing elements have secret connections and one cannot continue to exist without the other. On the path where the soul returns to the center waits the tree behind the tree and the revelation of a secret unity behind opposing views. Those who settle for a single view of life embrace only half of the living tree.

The search for knowledge is not intended to end at the same level where it begins. The struggle that began at the Tree of Division intends to bring forth a third element that only becomes possible after a clarity of contrast exists between opposing energies. The third element is the ripened fruit that also carries seeds for more growth. The conflicts common to any serious endeavor in this world secretly aim to transform the Tree of Division back to the unifying Tree of Life.

The soul is supposed to ripen during its sojourn in the garden of earthly suffering and delight. The Tree of Forgetfulness is supposed to return as the Tree of Remembrance once the soul awakens and recalls its calling in life. Those who argue mightily about right and wrong, good and evil in others often fail to tend to the inner conflicts. They sow bitterness and division while claiming to know the way back to the original garden.

Any genuine path of return requires remembering the agreements the soul made before it entered this earthly realm where everything doubles at the threshold. No system or simple belief can fully awaken those inner agreements. At some point the oppositions and shadows within must be digested for the fruits of genuine knowledge to appear. Facing those inner shadows takes more courage and genuine faith than simply pointing out the shadows cast by others.

The entire journey of the soul seeks to find the center again. All wandering out into the world secretly aims to return to the center where essential things wait to be remembered. Be it marked by a tree or a cross, by a black stone or a white tabernacle, by a grand cathedral or a spiraling tower, by a simple pile of stones or an empty crossroads—the center remains the same. All journeys of the soul begin there and try to end there as well.

Each pilgrimage shapes a journey to the center, not just to some central monument, but also to the garden within. Each step a pilgrim takes in the direction of the outer goal also fosters a move towards the inner center. The real pilgrimage is occurring within where the tabernacle of the deep

Self waits to be found. One old name for the journey that begins at the Tree of Division and winds towards the roots of unity was the "difficult road to the center."

On a genuine pilgrimage arrival can happen anywhere along the way, even on the return journey. The middle of the pilgrimage appears wherever awakening occurs. Sometimes that involves reaching a famous shrine, at other times a side path or some backtracking leads to the moment of awareness. The road to the center remains difficult because the inner aims of the soul must be found; the outer paths either serve to open that way or to obscure its presence.

Those who insist upon one right and righteous way to travel to the center simply haven't been there. For arriving at the center opens the eye of the soul and reveals that all the ways and paths lead there. The differences between ways appear most evident and intense while one is still distant from the goal. Move closer to the inner unity and the differences and distinctions between outer paths diminish; reach the center for a moment and find the unity behind all the conflicted opinions, battling beliefs, and dividing attitudes.

RIPENING THE FRUITS OF KNOWLEDGE

The struggle between good and evil remains in the foreground of world events and dominates both literature and news stories. Meanwhile, the Tree of Life, the tree behind the tree, the tree behind all branches of knowledge and belief becomes increasingly obscured and threatened by the dust rising from both religious conflicts and fanatical political beliefs. In a sense, the recent history of the Western World involves a painful struggle to break the spell of the Tree of Division and find some way back to the tree at the center of the garden of imagination.

The Tree of the Knowledge of Good and Evil first appears in stories of the Garden of Eden. Eden means "place of delight" or "well-watered place," another reference to the garden at the center where the waters of life flow freely. When the waters at the center no longer flow and sustain the fluidity of images and ideas the original mythic sense has been lost and the symbols foster more division than unity.

When religious stories become literalized and harden into fixed doctrines they can lose the ability to tap the roots of imagination that gave birth to them. Instead of living symbols that speak to each person according to the shape of his inner garden, the story retreats behind a wall of doctrines and dogmas that must be believed and even fiercely defended to gain entry. Not that the bible story or other versions of it are the "wrong story," rather they only comprise a branch of the endless tales that rise from the stem of stories that stands at the center of the garden of imagination and earthly delights.

Once the Tree of the Knowledge of Good and Evil makes an appearance, it soon takes center stage. In many ways it's like the Tree of Forgetfulness that stands at the beginning of the tale of the soul and the divine twin. Like the tree of forgetting, it's a beginner's tree, a tree to begin things with, a starting point that points beyond itself towards hidden roots of unity and wholeness.

Adam and Eve become exiled from the garden of paradise for tasting the fruits of that knowledge and chewing on the troubling issues of good and evil. Yet the Tree of the Knowledge of Good and Evil is a branch of the eternal tree standing behind it at the center of the garden of paradise. Awakening to the oppositions and divisions in the world and in one's own psyche causes the paradise of infancy to disappear and initiates a longing for the original sense of unity.

PARADISE IS A PARADOX

Humans have a taste for knowledge, even a hunger for it; at times an irresistible desire to know and to understand. That's human nature, the part that humans bring to the natural world, a taste that was present at the very beginning before all the trouble started, only becoming evident once all the trouble started. Often, the desire to know is only equaled by a capacity to deny. Humans present a paradox to creation and there was paradox in the garden of beginnings as well.

Most people don't like paradoxes. Most want things to be either one way or the other with a distinct "here and now" and a "hereafter" that promptly follows it. Most people prefer a path to paradise that can be reached by following particular rules and believing in certain views. Yet paradise turns out to be a paradox and the original split that continues to divide the world was inherent within paradise as well.

Paradise first appears as a central garden of tranquil beauty, a place of ease and contentment. Instead of roaring and hunting, the lions lie down with the lambs; milk and honey flow everywhere and fruit hangs within easy reach. All is peaceful and satisfying. On the other hand, nothing much happens. It's hard to tell the lions from the lambs, and there are no compelling reasons to work at such distinctions. There's no growing old; apparently not much growing up either, not much growing at all.

There's no shortage of anything, except maybe intrigue or challenge, mystery or surprise. Paradise appears to be perfect, yet as is the case to this day, appearances can be deceiving. Everything anyone could want appears nearby in great abundance; yet one wrong move and everything becomes torn asunder. In paradise, exile is only one step away. Paradise presents both the original unity that people long for and the original split that continues to divide the world.

As long as the original couple stayed in the vicinity of the immortal tree everything was copacetic. Once they tasted of the fruit of knowledge the split between eternity and time, between god and humankind, between right and wrong became a conscious separation that has been seeded into all corners of the world ever since.

People continue to lament the loss of that paradise and Eve often receives the greater portion of blame for interrupting the tranquility of existence. Yet the old meaning of *Eve* is "life" and *Adam* means "earth." In other words, the loss of paradise is necessary; that loss leads to life on earth and it sets up the longing for the divine that resides at the center of each soul on this earth. The story of the soul's encounter with the Tree of

Forgetfulness helps make that clear.

People keep forgetting that this world is made of trouble, that everyone gets into trouble, that those who try to avoid trouble both add to it and succumb to it in the end. Each time someone tells the old story the original couple goes for the fruit. How else could it be? How could the oft-repeated reaching for the branches of knowledge be a true crime? How could the god who created the entire situation, who planted the trees and set the serpent into its motion not know that trouble would be the result?

Those who consider the tale to be a simple warning or a caution against learning too much don't have much real faith in god. Either the deity knows what's going on or there is a lack of knowledge where the source of all knowledge is expected to be. Or else there's a kind of knowledge that the creator would like the creatures of the earthly paradise to explore.

Whatever the case, Eve and Adam, the original pairing of life and earth, had little choice. Before any unifying understanding can develop a clear division is required. Adam and Eve didn't know the difference between one another until they tasted the fruit of knowing in that way. If people consider that kind of union a sin they don't understand the desires that preceded their own life. Those who blame Eve and admonish Adam act like ungrateful children who can't find gratitude for the gift of life.

When it comes to knowledge people will get caught red-handed every time. The hidden meaning of the fruit of knowledge involves the recognition that everyone is divided within. All searching for an experience of unity and peace begins with the awareness of an inner split. The issue isn't that someone had the audacity to desire what the immortals know; the real issue is that most people refuse to know what they already know within.

Remember the tale of the tree of forgetting? Something keeps being forgotten despite intriguing stories being told over and over again. The knowledge that waits to be awakened resides in an inner garden. We can only know what we already know. Any learning is also a remembering. In reaching for a greater knowledge we awaken to the split within and then to the desire to heal it.

By now, the world has become so divided and conflicted that people might soon turn again to seek the deeper teachings in the old stories and let go of the dogmas and rigid beliefs that have grown attached to them over time. The Tree of Eternal Life can never be far away, yet it can easily be obscured by the enduring fascination with the oppositions and conflicts inherent in the world and in the human psyche.

It may be helpful to know that in the realm of myth and stories the beginning of a tale sets up the dilemma to be struggled with. A story that begins with the Tree of Division is secretly aimed at the Tree of Unity. It might also be helpful to consider that the issue of knowledge that divides and the longing for a return to union isn't back there, it's here and now.

EAST AND WEST MUST MEET

Many old stories place the Tree of Life and the garden of paradise somewhere in the Middle East, often in old Persia. *Persia* means "protected garden," and refers to the symbolic center where the water of life flows from the eternal tree. Following the paradoxical nature of paradise, the Middle East has become a place where religious and political conflicts threaten to draw everyone into an endless battle, or as some would have it an apocalyptic storm. For some people, taking old stories literally, actually seek to create a world-destroying conflict in order to bring the garden of paradise back.

The Middle East can be seen as the center of historical conflicts as well as the ancient place where the division between the Tree of Life and the Tree of Knowledge developed. In a wider sense, the Middle East also stands between the contrasting extremes of the Far East and the Western World. Seen that way, the Middle East is also the Middle West, the middle area that both separates and joins the East and the West.

Most enduring battles occur along a North-South axis. Countries repeatedly divide in two, the North and the South in the Irish "troubles;" North Korea and its southern twin; the two sides in the war in Vietnam and the American Civil War that still divides the states and underlies all elections. Yet, when the human world wants to really play with fire the opposition becomes East and West.

The Middle East continually erupts as the "trouble spot" on the earth and the troubles that erupt there attract the attention and involvement of nations far to the East and way in the West. The Middle East has always been the troubled center where the imagination of the Orient collides with the imagination of the Occident. Westerners call the area the Near East; those in the East could readily call it the Near West. The ancient tableland of Iraq and Iran can be seen as the dividing place and the troubled meeting ground of the Orient and the Occident.

Looking East from the Middle East leads to the Orient and "Oriental views" of life. *Orient* refers to "facing East;" more exactly to the moment of dawn. The East is the "place of the rising sun" and humans as well as many animals orient by turning towards the light of sunrise. Mythically, the Orient orients to the sense of an eternal dawn and endless cycles of existence. Many Eastern world views involve an "eternal return," a recycling of life, with death as an illusion and endless renewal as an expectation.

In some ways, death can be less troubling when viewed as in the East and considered as a pause in an eternal process of coming back to life again and again. The soul departs through the dark door of death but returns to the world again as the "wheel of life and death" endlessly revolves and one thing turns into the other.

On the individual level, notions of "karma" suggest that there's always some residue left over at the end of life, some unfinished business that delivers the soul back to the entry door with another soul errand to undertake. Oriental practices for centering can include "corpse poses" that involve the acceptance of one's own death as a way of being more fully in the breath of this life.

The traditions of the West include certain times for turning to the East. The sense of rebirth central to Easter Day celebrates the rising of the

"Son of God" after crucifixion and death and some time in the tomb of the underworld. It also coincides with the arrival of Spring when the whole earth becomes reborn after the dark days of Winter. Spring rituals can include dances around a garlanded Maypole as well as devotions at the Holy Cross, another version of Tree of Life when bereft of any branches.

In ancient stories Dawn was a goddess, the most beautiful and resplendent presence of all beings. One of her old names was "Eostre," the beautiful daughter who appears in the East and lifts the shroud of nightly darkness. Often she is accompanied by a troop of rabbits, whose rapid reproduction of life seems to mimic the procession of endless days produced by the eternal nights. Another symbol connected to the goddess of the eastern light was an egg, sometimes golden like the dawn. Life resides in the unseen golden center of the earth-shaped egg. Life hides within the inner darkness until it cracks the shell around it and bursts forth like the dawn.

More typically though, Western world views turn away from the dawn and fix upon the other end of the days on earth. Rather than an eternal return of the dawn of life through endless cycles of existence, Western myths tends to fixate upon an actual end of everything. For the West used to be called the "Occident." It's no accident that the West tends to view the world the other way around, for *Occident* means "facing the falling sun," or "sun-falling- down place." The West remains oriented towards the end, towards the shadowy remains of the day and the fall of the blood-red sun into the devouring mouth of the endless ocean of night.

In many stories the Land of the Dead resides in the West where the sun sets and leaves everything in the dark, implying that all is lost. Mythically, the West stares right at The End and dwells on the edge of existence with many stories of how the whole thing will one day come to a burning conclusion followed by endless darkness.

The Occident tends towards world views that include fire and brimstone and the incineration of the earth. The West tends to count on and even count down to the end of the world preceded by some celestial fireworks.

Even Western science seems intrigued with calculations of when a meteor might crash into the earth's atmosphere and set everything ablaze. Western notions of science tend to participate in older mythic orientations. Belief in science is one of the myths of the West.

The West also remains compelled by the Tree of Judgment that stands at the beginning of Occidental history. Western religions and sciences tend to see the origins of the world in historical terms rather than in mythical images that point to the eternal aspects hidden in this world. Increasingly, the origin stories shared by the three monolithic religions that grew on the Western side of the Tree of Life have come to be considered more as historical and moral doctrines than as truly mythical and psychological vehicles.

Brimstone means "fiery stone." Be it a punishment from an angry god or an accident of an accidental universe, the West tends to anticipate a fiery apocalypse that ends the whole drama and settles all conflicts with a great conflagration. Yet apocalypse refers to both uncovering and discovering. As conflicts throughout the world intensify and the darkness deepens, mythic imagination tries to enter again as it did once upon a time when everything was dark and the light of dawn had not yet shone. When the end seems near the beginning is also nearby, this period of unending conflicts and great uncertainty may be the context for East and West, beginning and end, to discover each other again.

THE FERTILE GROUND OF BEING

In the West, the individual must stand before a judging god, while in the East the sense of individuality can become lost in the seas of oblivion where dawn follows endless dawn. The West champions ideas of the importance and dignity of individual life and the possibility of personal redemption from the dark night of the soul. In the East the interest lies more often with the removal of the ego, the casting off of illusions and transcendence of all particular aspects of life.

The Occidental hero presents a distinct personality, often a tragic character doomed to be caught in the agonies of good and evil, of life and death. The Oriental hero is more an essence than a character, an image of something eternal barely covered with the sheath of human form. Two distinct and differing destinies appear from the opposite horizons of the world and each may have something to offer to the other as the world becomes smaller and all seems about to be drawn into greater and greater conflicts.

The potent mythological formula of the West takes a shape that pitches mankind onto the road of progress towards a one-time redemption that follows a final battle of good and evil. The extroverted, historical and factual nature of the agreement sets the stage for politically based "holy wars," as opposed to psychological and contemplative struggles within each soul.

Eastern imaginations take up the idea that eternity exists within each living soul and, turning inward in knowing ways, can lead to an awakening that transcends individual suffering. In awakening to the presence of the divine within, a person can reconnect to the cycles of eternity and the breath of the undying universe.

The West has a gift for stories in which the value of the individual becomes celebrated and life finds its meaning through the unique struggles of a singular soul who will never appear again in this world. Such stories help to raise consciousness of the importance of living the life given to its fullest extent. Meanwhile, the East tends to present the individual against the background of eternity and even the backdrop of the void. The point becomes less the celebration of the unique character and more the realization of the eternal presence and mystery that surrounds the soul.

East and West represent opposite world views and the increasing tension between the beginning and the end. Sometimes, fact and myth coincide; especially at the beginning when things have to become concrete and again at the end when myth tries to return and relieve the tension of overheated oppositions and entrenched polarities.

Each age must bring forth and shape symbols that combine the time-bound with the eternal. Each epoch must find again the river of life and cross over to the garden of eternal imagination. At certain times in the course of time the opposing orientations of East and West become important to each other. When it seems that the world might end, how a person and how a culture view the world have a greater effect than usual. When the end seems near it's time for the opposites to meet.

At this time, Eastern practices like yoga and meditation find their way into most corners of the Western world and Western notions of the uniqueness and importance of the individual life penetrate the East. Perhaps there can be an exchange of mythic imaginations that benefits each side so that the uniqueness of life becomes seen against the background of the eternal return, so that dawn and sundown, beginning and end can become connected again.

Ultimately, we take mythic steps to change historical conditions, reworking the ground of imagination to open things to the touch of the eternal again. When the opposites within the world become more revealed the trick is not to contribute to the widening split, be it the nuclear division that makes it possible to destroy the dawn and deliver an endless dusk, or the opposing religious views that battle over theories of good and evil and obscure the Tree of Life.

When all seems headed for disaster in a big way, the practice is to be able to hold East and West, beginning and end together. Sometimes East and West must meet, beginning and end must converse and exchange forms of knowledge that can lead back to the roots of knowing and the tree behind all branches of wisdom, the unifying Tree of Life.

CHAPTER 14

THE WAY TO THE GREAT WAY

As the old cloth of culture wears thin and the veil of "reality" lifts, underlying tensions become more revealed and more polarized. It's not just that the atom became split in the course of modern discoveries; the world also has become more intensely divided. On one hand the future of the world has become less certain, while on the other hand people become more absolutist about religious beliefs and secular ideologies.

As the uncertainties of life have become more pronounced, fundamentalisms of all kinds have intensified. The twin offspring of the nuclear age seem to be Uncertainty and Absolutism. The sense of a final end being near exaggerates the tendency to split things into polar opposites: here and the hereafter, now or never, the "true believers" and the "infidels," the righteous and the damned.

Theology has always walked a borderline where pathology also prowls. When religious stories lose essential connections to the mysteries they point at, they tend to collapse into literalism. Soon spiritual paths become pathological dead ends. Soon prophecies are taken as fact and facts are rejected unless they support the prophecy and substantiate the sanctioned texts. Faced with increasing uncertainty throughout the world and lacking genuine internal stability, political and religious groups often act out growing insecurities.

Religious doctrines and dogmas tend to restrict instincts as well as imagination and readily become a festering ground for apocalyptic conversions and reversals. Thus, the paradox of "religious terrorism" appears where doctrinal ideas and rigid beliefs suppress the instinctive and imaginative flow of life. The more restrictive the attitudes, the more destructive and negative the apocalyptic and messianic energies engendered.

The religious instinct in people won't go away; people are aimed at something divine from the beginning. Not only that, people need ways to enter life more fully, to find paths that lead to greater awareness. All religions arise from a core imagination of the divine and all can lead to some awakening of the inner life. The issue isn't the presence of religious urges and beliefs, but the lack of imagination that occurs when one belief insists upon dominating other views.

There have always been many ways to seek for the presence of the divine. That's the meaning behind the myriad of spiritual practices and religious approaches. That's why there are so many gods and why some of them have many arms. Like the eternal tree, the divine branches out in many forms in order to be near everyone and in order to be found more readily.

Everyone enters this world on an errand for god; it's just that the errands and the gods can appear differently once the journey through time has begun. The closer people move to the divine the nearer they are to the center. At the center many conflicted things can become clear; yet even a meaningful path begins at a specific point on the path and usually with a specific attitude for seeking the divine.

It's like the old Hindu story of the young devotees who were trying to learn all they could about god and the meaning of life. One of them insisted that moving closer to knowledge of the divine required awakening a great inner desire. Not only that, but the divine must be pursued with complete commitment and an all-out effort. His friend argued that even a great effort could be aimed in the wrong direction. Simply making an effort couldn't be a dependable approach. He felt the opposite way, that only in surrendering one's will and egotism could a person be sure of finding the way. He insisted that a systematic removal from all desires and distractions was the only way to proceed.

For one, committing completely and doing your all was the only way to go; for the other, withdrawing and "non-doing" was the sole answer. Neither would budge from his opinion and neither could convince the other; so they went to a teacher for help.

The believer in supreme effort spoke first, asking the teacher if it were not true that risking everything and giving all would move a person closer to god. The teacher replied that it was certainly true, such commitment and effort were bound to have an effect. Then the champion of non-doing spoke. He argued cogently that only by withdrawing from desires and learning to surrender to something greater than oneself could a person approach the divine state of stillness. The teacher immediately agreed with that approach as well and stated that the young seeker was speaking truth.

A third student happened by during the discussion and stopped to listen to the impassioned spiritual arguments. Suddenly he entered the conversation. He argued that the two positions were exact opposites, so both sides could not be correct. Impressed again, the teacher responded that he also spoke the truth. Now, there were three truths each of which contradicted the others; yet each was also true in some way.

Take it as a warning or take it as a lesson; take it as neither, or both. Take it as the kind of story found when people in this world begin seeking ways to awaken and find paths to the divine.

There was some truth in the fervent attitude of each young seeker. There are people who can only grow by giving all they have. Others turn the other way and must learn to surrender completely or else lose their way entirely. Yet others must find a third way that recognizes both intensities and cleaves a middle path between them. The teacher's way of seeing it was another form of truth. He saw more than one true way.

At the beginning of a spiritual path distinctions become critical. The beginner needs enough conviction to risk setting off and leaving familiar things behind. Support from like-minded people may also be needed if the risk of transforming be truly taken. Everyone one must begin the search in a particular way, usually amongst those who see the path in the same way. Farther along, things may appear quite differently.

Once underway, a greater surrender will be required or the path won't open wide enough to reveal hidden things. Along the path there are bound to be obstacles and conflicts, inner and outer. There are even stretches with no clear way at all. Always, there are doubts. If the students had no doubts there would be no argument and no need for an experienced teacher.

Doubt involves the practice of holding two opposing views at once. That tension may bring some uncertainty, but it also provokes true questioning and growth. Those that have no doubts tend to dig in where the paths of true learning have just begun. In language, doubt and dubious share common roots. In practice, a way that rejects doubts usually becomes dubious when difficult inner issues arise.

The teacher in the story was waiting for the students at an intersection where one way encounters another. The teacher had no choice but to recognize the truth of each way and even validate the necessity of the arguments that arise once people enter upon a meaningful path. Obstacles and arguments, fears and doubts are part of seeking; sometimes they block the path, sometimes they are the path.

Each path may be great in its own way, yet there is no direct route to the divine. The center connects all the paths of desire, longing and devotion; yet that cannot be known until a person suffers some detours and travels far enough along a chosen path. Each path can lead to the unifying center, but only if followed far enough.

Near the center all true paths enter a common ground. In the presence of divine connections things can be seen that were invisible at the beginning. The farther one stands from the unifying ground, the wider the differences between spiritual paths appear. In the initial steps along the way people can become dogmatic and overly determined about a path they have just entered or a vision they might have received.

It's like the temple where some disciples became intrigued with gambling. At night, after all the tasks were done and all the religious duties completed, the young seekers would gather and gamble in the dark. A certain advanced student took exception to this wicked practice that violated all the rules of the sacred precinct. He went directly to the spiritual leader of the place and lodged a formal, if not meticulous complaint.

The master listened to the whole thing, but did not become upset or insist on some punishment; not even a tightening of the rules. To the surprise of the advanced student, the spiritual teacher remarked that at least something was being accomplished since they were staying up all night. Perhaps if they continued on that path they would learn why people remain awake and undertake vigils of attention and contemplation in the night.

There are many ways of waking up; staying awake all night is one of them. A real path always involves some kind of a gamble. Any genuine seeker in this game of life must continually up the ante. Often, those who have advanced to some degree become the most dogmatic about how to act. They prefer to protect their position and insist upon fixed attitudes as well as rigid doctrines. That's usually a sign that they have stalled in their own progress and seek to mask their failings by condemning others.

Meanwhile, there's no help for it, each must start somewhere and everyone stumbles along the way. Those that claim otherwise are hiding something or doing something forbidden to them in the middle of the night. A path can begin anywhere that a person risks the comforts and security of the little self, but it can only continue where the deeper Self gains more acceptance. Accepting the deep Self within tends to increase one's tolerance for the presence of the little self in others.

NOT SINGLE-MINDED, BUT UNDIVIDED

The idea is not to be single-minded, but to become undivided. It's a common mistake to confuse singularity of vision with wholeness of being. People can hold a single idea or a single-minded vision of reality while projecting their inner conflicts and shady feelings onto others. This splitting is a fundamental mistake. Often fundamentalism grows exactly where a person divides within. One part of the person becomes devoted to the letter and rule of the law, while the other side judges and castigates whoever seeks in a different way.

Those who proclaim to the outside world that they have found "the one and only way" often hide a division within. How many religious leaders become exposed for some hidden behavior that they condemn in others? Better to become undivided inside while allowing a diversity of beliefs and approaches outside.

The "individual" is one who encounters the opposition within and suffers with it until inner unity develops. Only those who become brave enough to face the darkness within become generous enough to forgive others caught in a darkness of their own. Any forgiveness begins within one's own heart, otherwise forgiveness becomes a pretension and secretly another form of superiority.

Those who see everything one way soon come to believe that everyone must see things their way. Religious fanatics do that; certain worldly leaders do it as well. Each may have only a part of the picture, yet claims to have the whole answer or the only way to proceed. In this world anything can become a path if followed far enough. For each way secretly tries to reach the great path and universal way that leads beyond common conflicts. Only after reaching the crossroads where the many paths cross does the vision open wide enough to see that all ways can be "ways to the Way."

If the way to the center were easy to find and subject to control, it wouldn't be the Way. If the path could be found by simple belief all the true believers would be opening the doors and windows of their hearts with gestures of true compassion. They would find the common value in the words "Jesus was right" and "Moses led me along" and "Mohammed opened doors in my heart."

When the great way opens even for a moment the path between mind and heart widens. The heart begins to find the thought of unity buried within it and the mind feels in subtle new ways. Finding the great way requires a willingness to surrender again and again; not simply to bow one's head in the same old way.

THE YOUNG WOMAN'S PRAYER

It's like the story of the young woman on her way to meet the person she loved more than anyone else in the world. Her mind and heart became united while on the path to meet the one who ignited love and devotion within her. It happened that her path took her into a courtyard often used for prayers. And she happened to enter that place at the time when certain people stopped their worldly tasks in order to remember god and pray.

A certain man made his prayers in that courtyard several times each day. He was devoted to his faith and carefully followed the practice of praying to god at specific hours. The man of god had just begun the recitation of his prayers when the young woman entered the courtyard on her errand of love.

There was a local rule against interrupting those who took the time to pray; but she walked right past the one kneeling in prayer and didn't seem to notice him at all. The passing of the young woman distracted the holy man from his prayer; he became frustrated and unable to proceed in the usual manner.

After meeting with her beloved, the young woman returned along the same route. As she passed through the courtyard again the holy man interrupted her passage. He asked, "Don't you know that it is against the precepts to interrupt a person who is praying to god? Are you unaware of the fact that people use this courtyard to pray and that in passing through here you interrupted my prayers? Do you not know that there are penalties for these transgressions?"

The young woman apologized immediately for interrupting the prayers of the holy man. Then she asked a question of her own. "What do you mean by prayer?" The holy man answered, "By prayer I mean my attempt to speak directly to god. Prayer is a spiritual conversation with the divine that should not be interrupted by the comings and goings of the secular world."

The young woman spoke again, "I have another question then. If you were talking with god at that time how come you noticed me; while I, on my errand of love, never noticed you at all?" The silence that spread over the entire courtyard served as her answer.

It seems that when love is omitted prayers become easily interrupted and even misdirected. On the other hand, where love is involved every action can become a prayer to the beloved. It's not that love and religion must be at odds with each other, rather that wherever love and genuine devotion appear, there the divine will also be present.

The self-proclaimed holy man preferred rules and prescribed attitudes to a genuine conversation with the divine. He forgot that the divine can enter anywhere and in any disguise. It's an easy mistake to make regardless of the spiritual path undertaken. Were he able to see beyond the local pattern of belief, he might also perceive how the young woman was carried by the prayer of love. Were he not so dedicated to a single-minded view he would have glimpsed the presence of god in the devotion of the young woman.

In the courtyard where people entreat the divine the young woman was more devoted, more committed, more carried on the feet of spirit. She was close to some presence inside and could not be distracted from her errand.

Some might argue that the young woman was only on an errand of earthly love; only moved by some human form. Remember, a person must begin somewhere and giving one's heart fully can open ways of surrendering to greater and greater things. Doesn't the divine dwell in the hearts and minds of other seekers? Lovers may think that they only seek each other, but the one who sets them seeking is never far from their loving.

Where duty becomes love, a greater and deeper faith has blossomed. For the deepest meaning of belief refers to being loyal to what the heart already loves. As people used to say, "What the heart loves is the cure." The cure for healing the wounds and conflicts between faiths and systems of belief involves awakening to the unique ways that each heart carries devotion and love. When simple belief transforms into wisdom, raw passions can become a compassion that trusts what resides in one's heart and even in the hearts of others.

TWO MISTAKES ALONG THE WAY

On the way to the Way two great mistakes are often made. One mistake involves including everyone at the point where some subtle or esoteric issue requires careful learning before proceeding in a good way. The other common error involves becoming exclusive in ways that reject the sincerity of others while controlling too firmly the spirit of those already involved.

In this world where one thing can turn into another, the dream of making a sanctuary for spirit and refuge for those who truly seek can easily become a nightmare of rules and restrictions that keep people from the presence of the true spirit. The setting of stones can lead to fixating on certain ideas, soon there is only one approach allowed and one understanding to profess.

The instinct for building temples and churches sets up the dangers of establishing fixed ideas, even harboring blind beliefs. Sometimes the temple is a valuable indication of the Way, and sometimes a temple is in the way. Sometimes a church is constructed in the middle of the way and its brick-by-brick dogmas become obstacles to truly learning and blocks to really finding.

Sometimes a path requires some exclusion before it can open in greater ways; sometimes everyone who comes to the door must be welcomed with open arms. Distinguishing between opening and closing the doors of spirit becomes a necessary practice along any meaningful path. Temples, cathedrals, and mosques can be indications that the divine is nearby; yet they can also be mistaken for the place of arrival.

Once a myth or symbol becomes codified, fixed in stone, and firmly orthodox it loses its capacity to deliver the flow of imagination and vitality that it originally possessed. It becomes a "matter of belief" and soon it is only the belief that matters. Orthodox combines the Greek *orthos*, "right, true or straight" with *doxa*, meaning "opinion," "a way of praise," or "how to seem." Thus, an orthodoxy praises certain opinions and seems to provide all that is needed to go the right way.

The opposite of an orthodox approach often becomes a heresy. Yet, heresy comes from a Latin root meaning "a school of thought or philosophical sect." The nearby Greek root *hairesis* means "to take or to choose." A heretic chooses a different opinion or school of thought than that of the orthodoxy. Some heretics act out of simple rebellion or a new form of confusion. Yet some depart from the orthodox path in order to open doors to the living spirit again.

In that sense, each true seeker must become a heretic along the way in order to go beyond the little path originally entered. Wasn't Jesus heretical in the temple of the money changers? Didn't Mohammed break the mold? Didn't Joseph follow dreams? Didn't Buddha reform both Hindu and Jain practices? Those whose footprints are revered and followed walked in unique ways. All the orthodox ways derive from those who went their own way in order to find the great Way again.

THE PATHLESS PATH

In the long run, the path must be continually remade, made anew. If the same way of knowing found at the beginning could take one the whole way, there would be no reason to go at all. If the footprints of others could be followed the entire way there would be no reason to have new seekers. If two people always agree, one of them is unnecessary. Each path requires that those passing through make the way again.

A person can begin with the local and orthodox ways, or else borrow some foreign practices; after all, seekers must actually seek. Any path that has footprints of the old seekers can lead a long way. Yet at some point the path seems to disappear; this is true for the indigenous person as well as for the cultural orphans and spiritual wanderers.

On the way to the Way the footsteps of those who went before inevitably become obscured. This doesn't indicate that something has gone horribly wrong. Eventually, one must make one's own way in order to keep finding the way to go. At critical junctures the footprints of others disappear and a person must enter the "pathless path."

An old saying reminds us: "While preparing for the journey, you own the journey; once you step onto the path, the journey owns you." In order to continue on our path we must come to know who we are in essence. Only then can we learn the difference between simply believing in the religious experiences of others and actually "knowing" what to do in the present moment.

Truly seeing and simply believing can be two different things, especially when blind faith enters the picture. Those who follow blindly have little faith to begin with. When the inner eyes don't open wide enough people can feel threatened by visions of the divine that others have. Not really knowing what to believe in, they shift to condemning the beliefs of others as ridiculous or evil. Yet evil, like beauty and truth, tends to be in the eye of the beholder.

AN ELEPHANT ON THE WAY

Remember the tale of the blind men who encountered an elephant for the first time? This was new territory for them. They all gathered around what they could sense, but could not see. It was clear that a living being stood before them; it was enormous and they could smell its presence.

Each reached out to touch what was before him and found a different part of the great being. In the Braille of their searching each touched something of consequence and each felt some definitive and distinct qualities.

One blind fellow held the trunk of the elephant and declared that the wondrous being before them was like a tube that had a capacity for spraying cooling waters like a fountain. For him the unseen presence was fountainlike: firm to the touch, but soothing, and refreshing. Another, holding the tail end, had to disagree and insist that this was a "rope being" with a tendency to flail at anything that came near it.

Meanwhile, the one touching the great tusks had inner visions of carved statues and smooth body forms. Another leaned against a huge leg and described it as a pillar of a temple. Each held to what was near at hand and each developed a certitude based on what he happened to encounter and feel. Each named the presence based upon the initial experience. In becoming fixated upon a part of the unseen presence before them, they all failed to grasp the whole.

Secretly, they are all in touch with the same essential presence. Yet unless some greater knowledge enters the picture they might argue forever with each view being substantiated by limited experience and a need to be correct at the outset. In the common blindness the unity before them cannot be discovered, even though they are willing to touch something greater than themselves.

Strangely, the elephant can't help much either, as it represents a different order of being. Secretly, the animal presence holds all the conflicting believers together, yet they remain unaware of how the parts are connected. The elephant is one of the Intermediaries, a presence that can be felt, a hint of a unity beyond ordinary sight. It can only offer each seeker the part closest to him to begin with.

The common blindness involves confusing the parts with the whole, and the openings provided by the various religious and societal ways with the great Way. The situation would be simply humorous or entertaining were it not that people develop religious intensities and fervors of belief that cause them to reject any way but their own. How else explain how spiritual seekers and religious devotees can convert to fanaticism, absolutism, and even terrorism? In the modern world blindness takes the form of the many "isms" that develop within mass cultures.

It's only a little story and the great religions, political movements, and belief systems include elaborate and intricate forms of knowledge. Yet there is something to the notion of the blind leading the blind. There's something to the sadness that descends with the full realization that "in the kingdom of the blind, the one-eyed man can rule."

Seeing things only one way is a form of blindness. When people insist upon seeing in one-sided and single-minded ways, everyone becomes more blind to the universal need for acceptance, compassion, and forgiveness. The darkness of the dark times doesn't only come from the outside.

In this world of endless incarnated things, in this realm of the five senses and the myriad of beings, even god must become manifest in multiple ways. Once the inspiration for creation begins, the one god, the original deity becomes many gods. The paths back to the unifying source become manifold as well. Spirit may be One, but it comes to be known only through the many.

It's like love which draws people of all shapes and sizes together and even entwines those who inherit mutual animosities and opposing religious views. Once a person falls in the fields of love all the rules are broken; the person become open and exalted in ways that transcend the local issues and historical antipathies. Love, like genuine devotion, will find a way.

People may struggle with ideas of love and question the ways of love; after all it does upend everything and can obliterate all reasonable arguments and certified plans. Yet the love disorder only points to a greater order that supersedes reason and proves the presence of something beyond. The lover has lost his head because he has found his heart and the heart has its own reasons; reasons that have to do with the original agreement made with the divine before entering the calamities of history and the conflicts over the mystery before everyone.

Once love or beauty or genuine knowledge awakens the seeds planted in the inner garden it becomes possible to see truth in ways that are foreign; even in ways that are contradictory to each other. Remember the young seekers who argued over the passion of commitment and the devotion of surrender? They were each in touch with a part of the truth and those contrary passions could move them onto paths that might later open to the center if they continued their searching and questioning.

It's possible that the one dedicated to striving and giving all he had might one day have to surrender all of that and more. The other, who practiced surrender and advised others to go that way, might also have to surrender that approach. Sometimes people must surrender to the passion that awakens inside and allows them to make a leap that changes everything.

Meanwhile, many of us overestimate how far we have come along the way. Having struggled a bit and faced some fears, the tendency to dig in and protect what has been found can develop at any point along the way. It's a small step from having a vision that opens the way to losing one's way and becoming blind again. Sometimes we are chasing spirit; sometimes it is trying to catch up with us. That's why they say, don't trust ways, they always change.

It's like the group of students who were arguing fiercely. Each contradicted whatever argument the others developed and they all indulged in those feelings of superiority that feed certain forms of contention. Yet when their teacher passed by, they all turned suddenly silent.

The teacher asked what all the conflict and commotion was about. After some reluctance, the students admitted that they were arguing over the presence of evil in the world and whether the Evil One was trying to deter them from their work and their progress in life.

The teacher became silent for his own reasons. After a moment he said, "Don't worry too much and don't argue over the views about and the causes of evil in this world. At this point you have not progressed enough or moved close enough to your genuine selves. At this point you remain quite unripened, not sweet or good enough to attract the Evil One. At this point he is not chasing you at all; rather it is you who are still chasing him."

If the great Way is to be found again some ripening of the current situation will be required. The common habit of ascribing evil to any who see things differently or use other approaches to life has become more dangerous since humans possess the power to divide atoms and explode the world. Fears that the end might come soon tend to increase the blindness and darken the darkness that's all around.

Old paths and new ways of seeing must both be tried. For any path might lead to the central garden where life renews, although only if followed far enough and only where the individual soul faces the darkness within and finds some healing there before telling others how to go.

It's as if the whole world has entered a crossroads that ancient cultures encountered many times before. The choices made at those times and the visions found by those old seekers opened surprising ways to learn and grow. Some of those ways continue now and even travel from one land to another. It seems to have become a time for seeking the great Way again and a time for giving up the arguments over the sources and causes of evil in favor of practices that ripen the inner fruits, that heal the deep divisions, and awaken the genuine projects of the soul.

CHAPTER 15

THE RETURN OF HEALING

There's an old Native American story that describes the origins of healing ceremonies and the relationship between people and knowledge and the earth. It all started long ago, back when the heavens first became separated from the primal waters allowing the earth to form in between. Once there was some solid ground, the One Who Made the Earth fashioned some people and placed them upon it.

Like everyone who has arrived on earth since then, the First People found themselves living in a particular place that had specific conditions. For various reasons those early ancestors didn't like that first place at all. They didn't rest well there and they didn't dream well either. Since it was so early on, the creator could still speak to them directly. Noticing how the restlessness and lack of sleep made the people more fearful and confused, the One Who Made the Earth advised them to take a journey and seek a location more suited to their needs.

That was enough encouragement to set the First People wandering about, and people have been wandering off ever since. For that matter, people have had trouble sleeping as well and some say that contemporary people no longer have big dreams. At any rate, what happens at the beginning becomes an ongoing pattern and people still feel the urge to wander as much as they feel the instinct to settle down. The grass is always greener somewhere else and at the same time, there's no place like home.

Eventually, the First People found a place that seemed to suit them. They began to sleep deeply and soon were having big dreams. They rested well and began to dwell in that place in a good way. They learned from that place and became attached to it. Soon, they called it their homeland.

After a time, two of those First People became ill and day by day they became weaker and weaker. The other people did nothing to help them because it was the very beginning and they didn't know about sickness. No one knew anything about healing. The One Who Made the Earth spoke to the people again, saying: "Why don't you do something for those who are suffering amongst you? Why don't you say some words over them?" But the people had no knowledge of healing or of curing ceremonies; so nothing happened and the sick ones became weaker as if life were draining from them.

Then it happened that four of the people left the village at the same time. They set off at dusk and each took up a position facing into the darkness of the oncoming night. Once the dark had swallowed all the light, the One Who Made the Earth spoke to one of those people facing the dark. "Everything on this earth has the power to cause its own kind of sickness or make its own kind of trouble. But it also must be known that for each illness the earth has a cure; that for each kind of trouble on this earth there is also a remedy to be found."

The person who heard these words now understood that knowledge was available and that healing was possible on this earth. That's how it started; the possibility of healing began at the same time that knowledge entered the world. Healing and knowledge began together and remain connected in essential ways. To this day those two travel together, so that knowing the illness is the first part of curing it and facing the darkness at the edge of awareness is the first step in knowing anything.

The one who had received the knowledge about healing shared it with the others who stared into the darkness. Once they understood that a cure was possible, those four people went out and faced the darkest parts of the night at the end of each day. The next night the one facing to the East suddenly began to chant a prayer and sing a song. On the following night, the one facing South began to drum and play a lightning song. On the third night, the one to the West began to chant a prayer. On the fourth night, the one facing to the North began to drum and play another lightning song.

People ask: Did those songs come to them from the outside world? Or did the songs arise from the darkness within them? The answer is: Yes. The songs and rhythms seemed to arise from inside, just as they arrived from outside. The One Who Made the Earth seemed to give them these healing songs in both of those ways as knowledge and rhythms came to them spontaneously. Even now, knowledge involves both the inner realm and the outer world; genuine healing includes both as well.

The One Who Made the Earth came to those four standing people and spoke again: "Why don't you go to those sick people and sing for them and say words over them and help make them well?" So the four went back to the village. They brought the sick people right to the center of the village and invited everyone else to join them.

They spoke words over the ones who were ill and sang the songs they had learned. They continued to sing and speak and play rhythms until the sick ones were restored and joined the dance of life again. Then everyone joined in as if some vitality had entered all of them; as if curing those who had fallen ill added to the health and well-being of everyone else.

After that, whenever any of them fell ill or lost their way, they would be brought to the center where everyone would gather around them. The trouble would become central to everyone and those who had knowledge would begin speaking and singing and playing while everyone else paid attention to the sick folks and to the way that healing entered and affected all involved.

It's an old story, the kind the elders would tell when times became dark again, when everything became threatened and mystifying illnesses seemed to appear out of nowhere. Of course, the elders liked the presence of the darkness; after all, their sight wasn't what it used to be. More than that though, they liked the way genuine visions came from the darkest directions. The dreams of the young come in the middle of the night and the visions of the elders come from consciously facing the dark.

Remember the old idea that suggested that the elders had to see seven generations down the line? That's called looking into the darkness. Becoming an elder involves learning to see in ways that go far beyond simple self-interest. In the old times the elders would have to consider the effects of their decisions and actions on unseen generations. Imagine the current leaders in most places today trying to do that.

The ancient notion of the elders had less to do with political power and social leadership and more to do with healing and deeper knowledge. It used to be considered that each genuine elder had some form of healing to contribute to this world. An elder was a person who had survived the troubles of his own life and had gathered some wisdom from facing the darkness within as well as what troubled others.

Since they knew that all people found themselves in trouble at some point and that darkness could overcome anyone at any time, they kept a fond eye out for the young folks who were always headed for trouble and had to enter enough darkness to dream their big dreams. The young ones were included when everyone gathered to face some trouble or try some healing. That way they found what kind of knowledge intrigued them and which of the old folks had something they could learn from.

In facing the darkness the First People found some knowledge and learned some healing ways. In facing whatever sickness was present they learned how to bring everyone together and make everyone stronger. Back at the beginning it was easier to see how the illness of one or two could secretly diminish the health of everyone.

No one desires sickness and illness, yet they are connected to the origins of knowledge and healing. That's the kind of knowledge that the First People found and the way seeing the Old Mind would have us find again.

As the world become more sick with conflict and subject to strange illnesses the Old Mind tries to return with the old wisdom that holds that for each trouble and sickness this earth also has a remedy or a cure.

The First People were "exemplary," they set the example for how to deal with sickness and troubles. We are the inheritors of their knowledge and their instincts for healing and surviving whatever troubles come along. If cures for the current woes of the world would be found, we could do worse than follow the example of those who dreamed the big dreams and found real knowledge about healing and making things whole again.

To be alive at this time means to be caught in a growing darkness that troubles the sleep of almost everyone. The issues of resting well and having meaningful dreams have returned with a vengeance. The darkness around us seems to grow deeper each day and reactions of blind fear and terror seem to increase as well. Unwittingly, modern people have arrived back at the place where the First People were when they recognized that something was quite wrong, but had no idea how to initiate a healing.

In many old traditions the sick or seriously troubled person would be brought to the center of the community. The illness of one or two was central to everyone when people felt more connected to each other. If the troubles of one were considered by all, people were less reluctant to bring the inner issues out. Beyond that, gathering together for the purpose of healing could open everyone in ways that reduced conflict and increased unity.

Often, a design would be traced on the ground representing the shape of the cosmos. The person suffering the most would be placed there, in the midst of everyone, in the middle of everything, in the center of the cosmos. In the old understanding the center was also considered to be the beginning, the navel from which all of existence flows. Bringing those who were on the edge of death or even at their "wit's end" to the center could also bring them back to the origins of life.

Symbolically, the troubled soul would be brought back to the place where its invisible umbilical cord could be reconnected to the source of all life. Since the beginning harbors all potentials, the sick one could draw upon the potency of the beginning in order to start over again. Healing wasn't simply a medical situation, but also an opportunity for renewal. All the troubles that eat away at people could be placed in the center that was also the beginning and therefore the place of renewal.

Often the words spoken to the troubled souls included creation stories, how things began when the earth first formed; back at the beginning before time began to wear people down. It was another attempt to bring the force of creation to those who felt life to be draining away from them. This kind of treatment was used for all kinds of ailments including mental troubles, the loss of soul, even depression, and the kind of trauma that plagues those who survive a war yet bring the battle of life and death back to their village.

Modern cultures have medical centers with remarkable technologies, but people often become isolated while there, and there's rarely enough singing and dancing to assist the return of vitality. The original knowledge of healing involved music and dance because life begins with sound and health involves inner rhythms. Remember Icanchu, who was able to stimulate life from the ashes by singing and dancing when it seemed that the entire world had been destroyed?

The beginning has primordial sound that still reverberates throughout the earth. The center contains all the potentials and potencies of life. The First People had the original knowledge that connects the center to the beginning and returns the potentials to the world. The Old Mind tries to catch up to us and even now the One Who Made the Earth whispers that knowledge exists and healing can be found.

For the ancient peoples as well as for the current inhabitants of this earth, healing involves learning to hold the ends and beginnings together. Just like stories, the beginning and end are held together by the drama in the middle. As soon as a story starts or a book opens, some people want to know how the tale will end. Yet the core of a story often contains the secret of its existence and the knowledge that it offers.

This earth story has darkness, knowledge, and healing in the middle. Facing the darkness leads to finding the necessary knowledge and ways of healing the situation. Ways to bring healing to the great conflicts and blindness that currently trouble the world might elude people unless they face the darkness of the situation. There are similarities between running towards the roar, entering into the ashes, and accepting the presence of the black dog of chaos. All stories attempt some kind of healing or revelation of essential knowledge. Yet all depend upon the presence of trouble and a willingness to enter the unknown.

Unlike ideas that suggest that enlightenment might be found by imagining figures of light, the old stories and teaching tales prefer the kind of knowledge and quality of healing that comes from visiting the darkness. Notice how going to the edge and facing the darkest places leads to awakenings as well as to finding the center again. The lightning of learning strikes where the darkness is deep. Despite their apparent simplicity, the old tales try to show the way to healing and surviving in this world.

Most people only recall the importance of the center after it has been thoroughly lost. Humans are that way. Someone must truly suffer, become lost, feel exiled, and on the edge before the longing for the center awakens. By now, the whole human tribe might be feeling that way.

Mythically, the center of one thing leads to the center of everything. Seen that way, the illness of one person becomes the ailment through which all that ails a community can be addressed. The wound in one person can become the door through which everyone can find the center of life again. Thus, the afflicted one becomes the center of the community and the opportunity for everyone to commune with the origins of life. That's why people used to say that the afflicted are holy; for they are one way that holiness and healing try to re-enter this world.

At the center, the original flow of energies, ideas, and images can return to life. If people connect to the origins, things might begin again. The center remains the source of unlived potentials, fresh starts, and second chances.

The original sense of apocalypse involved both an increase of darkness and chaos and moments of sudden clarity and revelation. On one hand there's an increase of depression, an atmosphere of fear and sudden winds of despair. There's an increasing danger of being devoured by huge energies that rise from the depths that are being churned as time turns over and things turn around. On the other hand, things turn mythic again and healing and knowledge become available right where the darkness gathers.

At the end of the Enlightenment, the primal darkness seems to enter awareness again through the discoveries that place dark matter and black holes as central to understanding the universe. Some say that dark matter constitutes all but three percent of the known universe. Of course, that makes it more of an unknown universe and seems to reintroduce the image of the First People turning to the darkness to understand the conditions of life on earth. At the beginning and again at the end the darkness of the world seems greater and closer.

Yet when facts and fears seem to point to an actual end, a hidden reversal is also underway. Facing the darkness can begin an about-face that brings the potentials of the beginning back into sight. We live in between times, in a time when the "betwixt and between" quality of life becomes more revealed, in a threshold time where endings and beginnings can change places rapidly.

Call it "initiatory time" where some things must be left behind, the way a person must step out of the realm of childhood in order to grow in a new way as essential levels of life must be encountered and learned from directly. Call it "revelatory time" as many things become uncovered and revealed, as if something essential is trying to re-enter the world; as if the collapse into materialism and historicism finally loosens and the subtle ground of myth and imagination waits to be found amidst the chaos and confusion.

It's as if the only way forward involves a step back from the competing disasters of the world and into the dusky realms of imagination where things take shape just before entering the glare of the daily world. Initiation was an old way of paying attention to what was being born and what was dying inside the moments of time that wait to be opened like letters from the world behind the world.

Those living in a particular era are not simply the denizens of history or the pawns of time, but also are the only possible recipients of the messages of eternity trying to slip into the world and sustain the discourse of the eternal drama of life and death and rebirth. The initiatory path opens whenever, wherever a person allows the intimations of the otherworld to enter and clarify what needs to die and be released from what needs to live more fully.

We live in initiatory times when each soul can feel more isolated amidst the dying breath of one world and uncertain about the umbilical pulsing of the next. It's not the lack of time that modern people suffer from, but a lack of connection to things timeless, mythic, and eternal. Like the moments of awakening to knowledge and healing experienced by those First People who willingly faced the darkness, the most real moments in life are timeless and mythic and open to the sacred.

Seen with a mythic eye, each moment is potentially momentous, each instant capable of opening before us as the dream-world does each time we fall into the timeless realms of sleep. The moment that is pregnant with eternity holds both the darkness at the edge of time and lightning sheets of knowledge entering the world. Through entering the moment symbolically, time breaks open, the past can be reclaimed to the present and the future returned to its potential.

Kairos was an old Greek term for the unique moment; the synchronous instant when all of time synchronizes as past, present, and future become available at once. Moments of kairos break open the blindness of time. When time cracks it opens to eternity and whatever we perceive becomes revelatory, even prophetic, as nuanced time reveals hidden aspects of the world and our own place in it. More than predict the future, genuine prophecy opens time to reveal the past as well. Genuine prophecy opens time and can reveal the past as well as peek at the future.

Kairos moments are ripe with elucidation and illumination as the plot clarifies instead of thickening. Hidden causes as well as intuitions of the next step become more evident. The storyline we are living in and living out becomes more visible and the inner thread of existence more tangible. Each momentous moment propels us further into the life-story we came to live when we first came to life. Such moments of awakening become "lived time;" time fully lived into leading to a life fully lived out. Such time is "ecstatic," it stands outside of time's relentless march and connects us to ancient ways of knowing and seeing.

An old idea posits that each cycle of day and night is equal to the entire world, for this world is made of days and nights. There is no other time except the time found in the exposures of the day and in the mysteries of the night. And each person has a moment of eternity waiting within the passage of each cycle of day and night. The way to find time again, even when it seems that there is no time left at all, is to find the moment of eternity waiting for you each day.

Such fully lived moments are linked in the soul; being outside of time, they remain eternally present, held in timelessness and instantaneous with each other. Another old idea suggests that what lasts after we take our last breath and depart from our time-bound bodies are those linked moments in which the soul was fully present, in which we awakened to things timeless and to the eternal threads in our lives. We live for such moments, live truly in such a moment, and die when such moments no longer open the world before us.

The Sanskrit word for such an awakened moment is "ksana." Although referring to the brief instant it takes to cut a thread, ksana also includes the endless cycles and circles of life. Like kairos in the Western tradition, the Eastern term refers to the eternal, favorable moment, the opportune time. Ksana involves a paradoxical escape from time by entering the given moment more fully. Entering the moment and living more fully parallels the spiritual passage from ignorance to illumination, from darkness to genuine vision.

Myth and dreams, love and sacred rites, certain shrines and wondrous places in nature can provide openings that break the spell of time and illuminate connections to the timeless realms. Such inspired moments and breaks in the temporal skin of the world not only interrupt time's relentless march, but can also effect a reversal of the spells of time. Through open moments time returns to its origins in eternity and mythic regeneration becomes possible. In such moments lost potentials can return and a return of wisdom can renew lost ideals.

Near the end "what goes around, comes around" and does so more quickly than ever before. "Re-cycling" isn't simply a practical solution, it's also a symbolic representation of the quick turnarounds that characterize life when the end seems near. As the veil lifts on the wounded cycles of both nature and culture the symbolic sense of re-viewing and re-valuing life can lead to both new ideas and the return of genuine knowledge and earthly wisdom.

Myth offers a genuine sense of re-creation, a "recovery" process through which we rediscover the Real world with its metaphysical, mythical, and imaginal shapes. Myth is a vehicle of knowledge, a means of liberation from the "spells of the obvious" and a source of renewal for exhausted time.

Myth has that strange quality that makes the most ancient sense of the world feel immediately present. Myth speaks with many languages of the beginnings and ends, of creations and destructions, and of the betwixt and between place where end and beginning trade places, where death and birth brush elbows as one passes on and the other steps in.

By facing the dark and the great unknown both knowledge and healing become available. That is the way of the earth and the way for the earthlings who truly participate in the paths of healing and making things whole again. As the collective sense of unity collapses, the uniqueness within individuals can become an essential source of unifying imagination.

The ancient Irish had a mythic sense for how to weave the world back into fullness when the center failed to hold and all seemed abut to fall apart and be doomed to darkness. When disorientation became the common shape of life and the four directions seemed about to be blown to the wind, then the unifying fifth direction would have to be sought. And it could only be found at the edges of the land, in the darkest places and along the misty cliffs where the otherworld plays hide-and-seek with those on earth.

If people are willing to go to a place that seems darkest to them, each would find something of meaning and value. For as the darkness feels closer, the threads of existence move near as well. In facing the darkness one finds again the enlivening thread of imagination connected to the original agreement made before birth. If each then turns back again and pulls the thread of life towards the middle of things, then each automatically contributes to regenerating the unifying center.

Pulling the various threads of meaning and purpose from the edges and margins of life back to the centers of culture imitates the pattern of bringing the afflicted to the center for healing. This "arc of return" could precipitate a return of the Old Mind with its primordial ideas and instincts for survival, help to convert the olders into elders while provoking a return of wisdom and a renewed interest in healing.

Amidst the current unraveling and flood of radical changes there can be no shortage of meaningful tasks and worthwhile projects. Whether it be at the edges of culture or in the haunts of nature, each of us can find gainful employment nearby if we are willing to face some darkness in order to find the right trouble to be in.

Seen that way the effort of each person initiates a reversal of the unraveling begun by the black dog of chaos. Each begins to imitate the Old Woman Who Weaves the World by facing the mess of things and bending to choose a thread and beginning to shape the living garment of reality in a new design.

That way no one has to "save the world" or pretend to do so. Each can play a part that reveals what is central to them and the sum of those parts can reconvene and regenerate and help renew life at the center. Since the center is also the beginning, the whole thing starts up again and the dance of creation goes wildly on until someone pulls another loose thread or the Old Woman of the World decides to stir up some new trouble.

ACKNOWLEDGEMENTS

I wish to thank all those who listen so openly and enter so fully into the inner territory of stories, for unless they are taken to heart, stories may not survive. Especially, I want to express gratitude to the many young people who bring the troubles of their lives and the anguish of their souls and trust in the medicine of stories to help.

The seeds of this book have been watered with the attention and nourished with the care of many people. I am particularly grateful to Jacob Lakatua who has been invaluable in helping to shape the imagination of the material, develop the design of the book, and fashion its cover. For guidance and support, both literary and personal; for inspirations and clarifications I am indebted to Peter Fedofsky, Rachel Bard, John Dally, Jack Kornfield, Soon Kim, Luis Rodriguez, Christine Armstrong, Lou Dangles, Orland Bishop, and Anthony Crispino.

Index

ABOUT MOSAIC

Mosaic Multicultural Foundation is a 501(c)3 nonprofit organization, a network of artists, social activists, and community builders. Mosaic formed to create cross-cultural alliances, mentoring relationships, and social connections that encourage greater understanding between diverse peoples, elders and youth and those of various cultural and spiritual backgrounds.

Mosaic means putting essential pieces together; forming a whole from separate, divided, even estranged parts. The process of finding, fitting and weaving together divergent, yet necessary pieces involves making new social fabrics from existing ethnic, spiritual, psychological and political threads.

Mosaic events draw inspiration from the traditions of many cultures and incorporate knowledge learned in the trenches of contemporary community work. Efforts at problem solving rely on locating the genius of the situation, as the unique spirit of each individual becomes a key to understanding issues and fitting the pieces of community together in new ways.

Current projects focus on youth at risk, 'genius based' mentoring and developing the 'arts of community' in diverse organizations and community groups.

GreenFire Press and **Mosaic Audio** are imprints of Mosaic Multicultural Foundation that serve to foster cultural literacy, mythic education, and multicultural community development. Proceeds from sales of books and recordings directly benefit Mosaic's work with at-risk youth, refugees, and intercultural projects.

For more information or to order additional titles contact Mosaic:
4218 1/2 SW Alaska, Suite H Seattle, WA 98126
(206)935-3665, toll free (800)233-6984
www.mosaicvoices.org ~ info@mosaicvoices.org

Books by Michael Meade

The Water of Life: Initiation and the Tempering of the Soul, Michael Meade

Mosaic Audio Recordings by Michael Meade

Alchemy of Fire: Libido and the Divine Spark, Michael Meade

Branches of Mentoring, Michael Meade

The Ends of Time, the Roots of Eternity, Michael Meade

Entering Mythic Territory: Healing and the Bestowing Self, Michael Meade

The Eye of the Pupil, The Heart of the Disciple, Michael Meade

Fate and Destiny: The Two Agreements in Life, Michael Meade

The Great Dance: Finding One's Way in Troubled Times, Michael Meade

Holding the Thread of Life: A Human Response to the Unraveling of the World,
   Michael Meade

Initiation and the Soul: The Sacred and the Profane, Michael Meade

Poetics of Peace: Peace and the Salt of the Earth, Michael Meade

Poetics of Peace: Vital Voices in Troubled Times, Alice Walker, Luis Rodriguez,
   Michael Meade, Jack Kornfield, Orland Bishop

Books edited by Michael Meade

Crossroads: The Quest For Contemporary Rites of Passage,
   edited by Louise Carus Mahdi, Nancy Geyer Christopher, and Michael Meade

The Rag and Bone Shop of the Heart: A Poetry Anthology,
   edited by Robert Bly, James Hillman, and Michael Meade

Books including contributions by Michael Meade

Rites and Symbols of Initiation, Mircea Eliade

Teachers of Myth, Maren Tonder Hansen

ALL PURCHASES FROM MOSAIC AUDIO AND GREENFIRE PRESS SUPPORT
WORK WITH AT-RISK YOUTH, REFUGEES, AND INTERCULTURAL PROJECTS.

For more information or to order additional titles contact Mosaic:
4218 1/2 SW Alaska, Suite H Seattle, WA 98126
(206)935-3665, toll free (800)233-6984
www.mosaicvoices.org ~ info@mosaicvoices.org